Homiletics

Karl Barth

Translated by
Geoffrey W. Bromiley
and
Donald E. Daniels

D0126607

Westminster/John Knox Press
Louisville, Kentucky

BOOK DESIGN BY KEN TAYLOR

First edition

Published by Westminster/John Knox Press
Louisville, Kentucky

PRINTED IN THE UNITED STATES OF AMERICA
9 8 7 6 5 4 3 2 1

Library of Congress Cataloging-in-Publication Data
Barth, Karl, 1886–1968.
  [Homiletik. English]
  Homiletics / Karl Barth ; translated by Geoffrey W.
Bromiley and Donald E. Daniels. — 1st ed.
      p.   cm.
  Translation of: Homiletik.
  ISBN 0-664-25158-7
  1. Preaching. I. Title.
BV4214.B313 1991
251—dc20   91-11976

Homiletics

Contents

Foreword

In 1963 *The Preaching of the Gospel* was published in English.[1] The book was based on student notes from lectures on preaching by Karl Barth. "I no longer remember when or where they were delivered," Barth wrote in a brief preface.

Now we possess a more complete version of Barth's *"Homiletik."* The text was drawn from records of a seminar Barth conducted at Bonn in 1932 and again in the summer of 1933 under the title "Exercises in Sermon Preparation."[2] The lectures were edited in consultation with Barth by Günter Seyfferth in 1965. A fine younger scholar, Dr. Donald E. Daniels, located the material and diligently prepared a draft in English. The task has been fulfilled by Geoffrey W. Bromiley, whose translations of Barth's *Church Dogmatics* and other works are, of course, well known.

Why publish a revised edition of Barth's homiletic lectures? The new edition adds much material, nearly fifty pages not found in the earlier work, as well as offering a more systematic, ordered presentation of Barth's thought. But still, why another edition?

Literary critics observe that the beginning of a story often prefigures the whole story—significant themes, central characters, even a kind of shape of things to come. In Barth's homiletic lectures we have an aston-

ishing disclosure of a young theologian at work form-
ing his later thought. More than any thinker in the
century, Barth linked theology and preaching: He pro-
posed that theology should be "nothing other than sermon preparation." Thus, to follow his deliberations on
preaching is to enter his theological world. Truly, here
we have a shape of things to come.

Barth's *Homiletics* is an even more useful gift to
preachers. Though many theologians have published
sermons—Augustine, the Reformers, Schleiermacher,
and more recently, Tillich—few theologians have
braved a work in homiletics. Barth, for a dozen years
a thoughtful pastor, never forgot his calling as a minister of the divine Word; he cared about the doing of
sermons.

How does Barth's work on preaching, delivered now
nearly sixty years ago, read in the 1990s? The central
thrust of his work, a call to fidelity to the gospel, still
rings true. And his radical insistence on grace alone,
particularly in matters homiletic, is as moving as ever.
As any preacher knows, preaching can easily become a
"work" designed to garner "effect," "conversion," or
"decision." But for Barth the word we preach is ultimately God's word, and the work we do is done by
grace alone. The preacher, justified by God's free grace,
speaks as a forgiven sinner to forgiven sinners and is
blessed (read: sanctified) by the gospel.

Of course, Barth's strong stress on the preaching of
God's Word leads him into some rather peculiar positions. He banishes "Introductions" from sermons, not
merely because in his era they had become pedantic or
trivial but because he will not allow the theological
notion of a "point of contact," some predisposition in
the self that will align with the gospel; for Barth there
could be no method of correlation. Likewise he con-
demns the whole idea of a "Conclusion" to sermons,
fearing that an ending will either be a "work" or a

weakening of the message of grace through trite sum-
mation or minor-key application. Perhaps the most dis-
turbing of Barth's polemics is his attack on "relevance."
For example, he regrets ever having mentioned World
War I in his own sermons. "Pastors," he wrote, "should
aim their guns beyond the hills of relevance." While
most of us would agree that a nervous, topical preaching based on ever-changing daily headlines may be
deplorable, are we willing to tell Allan Boesak or
Bishop Tutu to stop referring to *apartheid* in preaching—
particularly if we are white Reformed church people?

Probably Barth has been criticized most for his
strong, uncompromising biblicism: so strong that he is
willing to suggest that preachers risk no more than a
"reiteration" of the text lest, in interpreting, they
admix the scripture's message with their own cultural
thoughts. "The sermon," he suggests, "will be like the
involuntary lip movement of one who is reading with
great care, attention, and surprise." Barth clings to
scripture, guards scripture fiercely, and will allow no
dilution of scripture's divine Word.[3] Because of his
stubborn reverence for the Bible, Barth has been em-
braced enthusiastically by many moderating funda-
mentalists in recent years. He is unabashedly biblical
and seems to have had no awareness of the "her-
meneutic problem" that within a quarter of a century
would agitate the theological community.

Yet the section on scripture in Barth's *Homiletics* is
strangely moving. Those who preach the scriptures will
not be pontificating clerics or detached visionaries or
merely dull. For, again and again, the scriptures will
speak God's *new* word. "The proper attitude of preachers," Barth says, "does not depend on whether they
hold on to the doctrine of inspiration but on whether
or not they expect God to speak to them. . . ." Barth
calls ministers to "active expectation" and "ongoing
submission" in their study of the Bible.

One of the splendid features of Barth's *Homiletics* is the way in which he locates preaching in relation to the sacraments, baptism and the Lord's Supper. Barth does not deal with the church's worldly evangelism; he locates preaching in church, where the scriptural word of God may address the people of God, a position he had developed from his study of Anselm. But he affirms that church is where pure doctrine is preached and the sacraments rightly administered: "There is preaching in the full sense only where it is accompanied and explained by the sacraments." So, like Calvin in an earlier era, Barth insists that preaching and the sacraments be held together. He is scornful of the free-church Protestant neglect of the sacraments: "What kind of preaching . . . receives its prominence from suppression of the sacraments?" Barth pictures a Sunday service in which preaching occurs between baptism and Communion.

Karl Barth's lectures on preaching were delivered in the early 1930s. For more than fifty years, Barth has influenced Protestant homiletics. The world has changed; now even the most doughty Reformed Protestant people are apt to describe themselves as "post-Barthian." But Barth's thoughtful wrestling with homiletic definitions and issues is still worthy of attention because, to reverse Barth's own claim, sermon preparation after all is nothing other than theology.

DAVID G. BUTTRICK

The Divinity School
Vanderbilt University

NOTES

1. Karl Barth, *The Preaching of the Gospel* (Philadelphia: Westminster Press, 1963), trans. B. E. Hooke from *La proclamation de l'Évangile,* ed. A. Roulin (Neuchâtel: Delachaux & Niestlé, 1961).

2. In 1932 Barth, then a faculty member at Bonn, had completed his commentaries on Romans (1919, 1922[2]) and Philippians (1927). He had published *The Word of God and the Word of Man* (1924, E.T. 1928) and, above all, had shaped his theological approach in *Fides quaerens intellectum: Anselms Beweis der Existenz Gottes* (1931; E.T. *Anselm: Fides Quaerens Intellectum, 1960*) and *Kirchliche Dogmatik* I/1, *Die Lehre vom Wort Gottes* (1932; E.T., *The Doctrine of the Word of God,* 1936, rev. ed. 1975).

3. We should notice that though Barth does have reverence for the Word of God in scripture, he does not begin his definition of preaching with mention of the Bible. In the definition, scripture shows up in a subordinate clause and is discussed after Barth has defined several other criteria, for example, revelation, church, and ministry.

Preface

It might seem strange that at the very time in Bonn when Barth was immersed in historical and dogmatic theology, wrestling through to the definitive expression of the theology in the *Church Dogmatics,* he should take time to conduct a seminar on homiletics. Was this an excursion into an alien sphere? Was Barth seeking light relief from more serious business? Not at all! In his Safenwil days, when he had found himself a minister of the Word of God with little relevant training either theological or practical, the problem of preaching had been a primary driving force behind this quest for a new dogmatics. It was what finally prompted the momentous response of the *Romans* to Thurneysen's suggestion that the need was for "a wholly other theological foundation."

Even in his academic work, first in the biblical and historical fields, then in dogmatics and ethics, Barth never lost sight of his initial concern. Theology for him could not be an end in itself. It is not to be done in isolation from the church's supreme ministry. It is itself a secondary ministry. It has the servant role of critically and constructively testing the church's proclamation with a view to keeping it in tune with its function as testimony to the revealed Word of God according to the norm of the scriptural Word. The problem of the

sermon, the outstanding form of proclamation, still lay
behind what had now become Barth's main contribution to the church and its ministry. It is a tribute to the
urgency of his concern that he offered the homiletics
seminar along with a Calvin seminar, a Luther discussion group, and his lectures on dogmatics, and that no
fewer than 110 students elected to participate.

The substance of the course brings out clearly the
close relation that Barth discerned between homiletics
and dogmatics. His exposition and criticism of earlier
definitions of preaching introduce us at once to his
dissatisfaction with contemporary theory and practice.
His new definition expresses succinctly his understanding of proclamation as the third form of God's
Word in perichoretic relation to the first and second
forms. His practical counsel, especially the plea for ex-
pository preaching and his polemic against theme
preaching, testifies to his basic confidence in the nor-
mative prophetic and apostolic witness and his belief
that closeness to life, important though it is in the
sermon, must not be at the cost of closeness to the text.
The firm linking of preaching to the church and sacraments, the insistence on serious exegetical work (not-
withstanding ultimate dependence on the Holy Spirit),
and the recommending of both critical and theological
commentaries offer insight into Barth's breadth and
openness as he increasingly came to see the sermon in
all its theological dimensions.

Barth himself, of course, did not prepare these
homiletical materials for publication, though he gave
his approval to the venture when they were given their
present shape, as recounted in the Postscript. As regards the English version, we must be particularly
grateful to Dr. Donald E. Daniels both for his enthusiasm in promoting the project and for supplying a first
draft for the translation. It will be appreciated, of
course, that the relatively unpolished original posed

some problems in achieving the necessary balance between accuracy and readability. Readers should have no difficulty, however, in getting the sense of Barth's teaching and profiting by it, especially those who are themselves specifically engaged in the ministry of God's Word.

GEOFFREY W. BROMILEY

Pasadena, Easter 1990

Introduction

The generally theological character of the seminar title, "Exercises in Sermon Preparation," results from the fact that theology as a church discipline ought in all its branches to be nothing other than sermon preparation in the broadest sense. The title is not meant in any true sense to denote a separate theological discipline. The vital connections between the three main branches of theology—dogmatics, biblical exegesis, and practical theology—make this plain. On the one hand dogmatics, as the discipline that investigates the legitimacy of the church's function of ministry, receives its biblical norm from exegesis, and on the other it directs pracical theology with its special task to the sermon as such. Hence we cannot think of any one of these disciplines without the other two, nor can we speak of any of them in isolation without speaking of the others as well.

Only, then, as with this title we set ourselves in the living stream of theology as a whole can we inquire into the special meaning of the title relative to our present task. Three areas can then be considered: (1) the individual creative work of sketching and developing the sermon; (2) the more receptive and reproductive critical work of reading and listening to sermons and learning from them; and (3) the handling of dogmatic questions about the nature of the sermon as illustrated by past examples that deal with this issue. We shall tackle this third task first.

1
The Nature of the Sermon: A Historical and Dogmatic Sketch

I. Definitions and Criticism

1. DAVID HOLLAZ

We listen first to the voice of the late orthodox theologian Hollaz in a twofold description of the proper function of the *minister ecclesiae: "Minister ecclesiae officio docendi recte fungitur, (a) genuinum verbi divini sensum per legitima interpretandi media accurate investigando, certa eruendo et perspicue explicando, (b) verbum explicatum ad usum disdascalium et elenchticum, paideuticum et anorthoticum et paracleticum decenter applicando"* (The minister of the church validly discharges the office of teaching (a) by accurately investigating the true meaning of the divine Word through legitimate methods of interpretation, by surely exegeting and clearly expounding the Word, and (b) by fittingly applying the Word as thus expounded for purposes of instruction, reproof, education, edification, and consolation).

As opposed to Pietism and Rationalism, Hollaz can legitimately seek and expound the genuine meaning of the divine Word in orientation to dogma, and he can appropriately apply the expounded Word to the congregation by way of instruction, reproof, education, edification, and consolation. Hence this orthodox dog-

matician raises two problems and offers solutions to
them: that of the exposition of scripture and that of its
application to the congregation. In a subordinate sense
he also raises the problem of form. The twofold task
that he then poses for the preacher leads us to a question that we have to put to Hollaz. Has he correctly
depicted the position of the minister of the divine
Word by allotting him the function of grasping the
inspired sense of the Word of God as it is found in the
Bible and then passing it on to the congregation as the
entity that stands in need of various spiritual blessings?
Do we not have to seek a unifying point which on the
one side will avoid the paradox of the minister becoming an autocratic and complacent *dominus* and on the
other side do justice to the two main problems and also
to the subordinate problem of form, of the *decenter*
("fittingly").

2. FRIEDRICH SCHLEIERMACHER

The twofold task set by Hollaz may be noted again
in the dialogical attitude of the older Schleiermacher to
the text, which the minister must evaluate both in its
context, on the one hand, and with a view to the congregation and its trains of thought on the other.

In his practical theology, however, Schleiermacher is
not only in some sense the modified Hollaz of the eighteenth and nineteenth centuries but more brilliantly,
perhaps, when younger, yet consistently throughout
his life, he offers a distinctive account of the preacher's
task. For him preaching is only one of the waves, and
not the most important, in the surging sea of the congregation and its common feeling for the *universum*. It is
only one of the many obvious ways of expression of
this feeling. The younger Schleiermacher of the *Speeches
on Religion* might not have had the same sense of responsibility to the church as the older Schleiermacher of the

Practical Theology. The stages of music and mystery in worship, the ringing understanding of what worship is all about, and the analogy that he finds to the lyric, all point to the Romantic mother earth of emotion. The organist and the poet are the outstanding mediators between the concealment and the disclosure of feeling. In Schleiermacher it is only on this common basis that one can ask concerning the specific task of the sermon with its different shades of mood according to age.

For the thirty-one-year-old orator addressing religion's cultured despisers, the act of preaching itself was not the most important thing, but the speaker's awareness, when speaking, of emerging from the congregation, the absolutely republican city of God, and of returning to the congregation when finished. The sense of being a swinging pendulum protects the speaker against the arrogance of acting officially in virtue of a vocation, of deriving authority from any society, of trying to make prophetic announcements, of yielding to any human pride or conceit. It is the free moving of the Spirit that initiates the swinging of the pendulum, and this swinging takes place in sincerest unity with each and all and in complete equality, destroying every first and last and every earthly order. The preacher emerges from within the feeling that is common to all and speaks about the reality and mystery of the religion that is his home, about the unity of the subjective moment of feeling and the objective moment of contemplation, expounding a view of God, a view of the *universum.* With its senses engaged, the congregation follows the preacher on his travels through the *universum* and he injects his feelings into them, so that when he is externally one of them again and is silent, in an exalted mood the whole congregation realizes that it is in the very same theater of the very same feeling. The singing of the congregation is the great Amen to the preacher's speaking. It is a responsive wave, the echo of

his voice, a solemn affirmation that the preacher's
speaking was an expression of what was already inwardly well known and felt and possessed. How, then,
could the postlude of the organ not be understood as
a comprehensive expression of what had been set forth
and experienced afresh in the hour of worship, yet also
of the ancient treasure that was possessed already?

The older Schleiermacher differentiates between the
preacher as the organ of the church and the preacher as
the organ of the congregation. But he assigns to the
preacher a purely negative task. He must not be in
contradiction with that which constitutes the church's
unity; i.e., he must remain within the congregation. As
the organ of the congregation, however, he also has a
positive task. In his capacity as a living personality,
with the common impulses as his starting point, he has
to steer the bark of the congregation as it floats down
the stream of feeling.

In another passage—the last line of the first section
on the cultus—Schleiermacher finds that all perfection,
all proper regulation, and the true art of direction must
come from the innermost life of the clergyman personally with no mechanical aids. By way of analogy he
refers to lyric poetry. Lyrical composition, too, has its
source in a directly individual emotion, and it effects an
entry only insofar as the poet knows how to present it.
To be sure, all homiletics is called into question, yet not
as the beginning of a total questioning of all things
human, but only so as to honor the innermost life as the
wellspring of all grace. This innermost life of the individual personality, however, swings in the circle of the
congregation. And this giving and receiving, this flow-
ing back and welling forth, is the last word and the
supreme law of preaching. The *panta rei* of an upsurging
organism flows past us. The preacher takes the lead and
the chorus of many voices is religion.

The question arises: Where is the Word of God in

this immanent sea of feelings? Where is the ongoing seeking if all that is done is simply the expression of an inner possessing? What place is there for final waiting if the moving force is this-worldly possession or its lack, enjoyment or yearning? Not in any of these: Here is another world than that in which we are confronted by law and grace. It is another world than that in which God comes again and again. For it is the human world which as such flows out from itself and back into itself.

Quotations from Schleiermacher: "When one steps forward in front of others, it is not his office or call which allows him to do so, nor haughtiness or conceitedness by which arrogance flows into him. It is the free movement of the Spirit, a feeling of unity which the clergyman shares with each and everyone, in complete equality. . . . He steps forward to project his innermost self as a subject of shared observation that has been prompted by God, in order to lead them to the sphere of religion, where they feel at home so that he can instill his sacred feelings: He expresses divinity, while in holy silence the congregation follows his inspired speech . . ." (*On Religion* [New York: Harper & Row, Harper Torchbooks, 1986, p. 151]).

"The preacher is on the one side an organ of his church, on the other a representative of his congregation according to his position. As the organ of his church he must not be in contradiction with that which constitutes its unity. As the representative of his congregation he must have the common impulse as his starting point. These two things alone are his limits. By means of the influence of his living personality he must guide the common impulse and give it a specific orientation" (*Praktische Theologie: Theologische Schriften,* vol. 8, pp. 203f.).

"The clergyman has two viewpoints. He goes back on the one hand to the context of his scripture passage. But on the other hand he must also consider his congre-

gation and what it is used to. Because he is moving in
a free direction, he must be sensitive to the way in
which the congregation customarily thinks about the
matter. By its very nature the process is dialogical.
There is a dialogue with the text which the preacher
questions and which replies to him, and also with his
congregation" (ibid., p. 248).

"All perfection, all proper regulation, and the true
art of direction must come directly from the innermost
life of the clergyman himself with no intermediate
mechanical aids. We have here an analogy that is
obviously related to our theme, that of lyric poetry.
All genres fade in lyric poetry because lyrical composition has its source in a direct individual emotion and
it finds an entry only insofar as the poet can present
this" (p. 326).

For Hollaz the congregation and scripture confront
one another in the twofold relation of explication and
application with the preacher in the middle. The problem here lies in the distinctive position of the preacher.
One has to ask how he comes to assume (1) such an
authoritative position vis-à-vis scripture, and (2) the
middle position between the congregation and the
Word, if it allows him the authoritative position which
Hollaz simply takes for granted.

In contrast, Schleiermacher seems to have made some
progress at this point, for in him the dichotomy of
scripture on the one side and the congregation on the
other is dissolved in the unity of the Spirit-possessing
congregation. The authoritative position of the
preacher that is such a problem in Hollaz is now eliminated, for the preacher steps out of the congregation
and returns to it. His function, then, is one of service
rather than rule or attempted self-assertion. Yet precisely as one looks at Hollaz again, one has to ask
whether it is appropriate or not that, as in Hollaz, the
preacher again has a master's position as the mouth-

piece of the congregation. In addition a question arises concerning the relation between the Word of God on the one side and the preacher and congregation on the other. Finally, one has to ask (1) whether a sermon can really be compared, as in Schleiermacher, to exhaling followed by inhaling, and (2) whether the self-presentation of the pious feelings of the congregation is really preaching as Schleiermacher thinks. Schleiermacher, then, offers us an answer to the question of a unified understanding of the two given factors in preaching, the Bible and the congregation, but he then raises for us the question whether the Word comes from the congregation and whether it should not be viewed instead as the Word that comes to the congregation from outside.

3. ALEXANDRE VINET

The Swiss Vinet (professor at Lausanne) was a faithful disciple of Schleiermacher who is still influential even today. His starting point was the possibility of viewing homiletics as a special form of rhetoric. He was not trying to paganize homiletics, for, as we recall from Schleiermacher, natural life at its deepest level is already Christian and therefore true rhetoric is to be regarded fundamentally as homiletics. Rhetoric and the art of rhetoric consist of putting oneself into others' shoes and identifying oneself with their innermost being so as to be able speak for them. This innermost being in us is not evil but an advocate of the good, and it is the duty of Christian preaching to bring it to expression, so that during a sermon we are constantly reminded of our true selves. In this way rhetoric is filled with spiritual content, so that when the ideal of speech between people is achieved, i.e., when the innermost being of the one converses with the innermost being of the other, Christian discourse ensues. It is typical of

Vinet that a biblical text does not have to be the basis
of such discourse. Should it be asked whether a
preacher is addressing believers or unbelievers,
Schleiermacher would answer in favor of believers, but
Vinet, with a much more comprehensive dialectic, replies that preaching must always be for both. It must
lead those who do not yet know it to the truth of
Christianity, and it must explain this truth further for
those who already have a closer knowledge of it.

4. CHRISTIAN PALMER

Christian Palmer (professor at Tübingen), who died
in 1875, gives the following definition in his *Homiletik:*
"To preach is by living witness, and in the name of
God, to offer the salvation which appeared and is pre-
sent for human beings in the person and work of
Christ."

One might take up the distinction that is made here
between "appeared" and "is present." At first it seems
as if the only interest is in the objective side of the task.
Palmer would have us know, however, that a given
basis of Christian faith and life is presupposed which
also implies the more subjective side. The "offer"
denotes the establishment of the relation between the
objective and the subjective sides. This offer is made by
"living witness," i.e., by the utterances of a living personality. Since Jesus Christ appeared as a person, so his
work, i.e., the work of salvation, is to be offered by a
person. This person is not to be regarded, of course, as
a mere individual but as a representative of the congregation in which a spiritual-pneumatic personality is
set. The congregation gives this person the Word, and
as he addresses the Word to it, he is giving it back its
original possession.

Hollaz, Schleiermacher, and Palmer all have one
thing in common, namely, that the preacher is master

over what is to be proclaimed by him. In Hollaz a twofold dialogue takes place between preacher and scripture on the one side and between preacher and congregation on the other. In Schleiermacher, however, there is unity. Palmer at least hints at a new separation between scripture and congregation in a return from Schleiermacher to Hollaz. If we follow him in earnest, we end up with Hollaz again and the questions that we have to put to him. But if we ignore in Palmer the presence of (1) a Christian personality and (2) a given foundation, we are back with Schleiermacher, and we have to ask how the congregation comes to possess the Word of God and whether the preacher's offer is anything more than the offer of his own pious personality. Furthermore, if we were to take the idea of offering salvation strictly, we might say that overmuch is really ascribed here to the preacher. We might say, too, that in the offering of the Roman Catholic sacrament of the altar the tremendous claim that it can offer salvation is made much more soberly than in the Evangelical sermon because everything is there kept within the cultic and ceremonial frame of the liturgy. In all this we might indeed see a relation to the South German "Power Theology" of a J. T. Beck, which does not want to see words but deeds, facts, living events.

5. C. I. Nitzsch

In distinction from the ultimately unclear definition of Palmer, C. I. Nitzsch provides one that is precisely and thoughtfully formulated in all its members: "A sermon is the ongoing proclamation of the gospel for the edification of the congregation of the Lord, a proclamation of the Word of God through texts of holy scripture which takes place in a living relationship to contemporary circumstances through called witnesses."

a. The expression "ongoing proclamation" is coined in the context of the debate whether preaching is meant to be missionary or congregational. Faith should not stop giving utterance to what it has become inwardly. I believe and therefore speak. To this extent preaching is addressed to those outside; it is missionary. But the same faith is constantly nourished by the gospel which awakened it. To this extent preaching is addressed to those within; it is congregational in dialectical unity.

b. The speech of God and the deed of God form a unity inasmuch as Jesus Christ is the Word of God. The faith of the church proclaims Christ as he is communicated through scripture texts. What is required, then, is biblically related preaching, not prophecy.

c. The preacher's position must be as closely oriented as possible to that of the listener so as to illustrate the condescension of God.

d. To fulfill its commission, a Christian personality stands between God and the listeners, not in order to interpose its own individuality, but to serve. Preaching is impossible without a full believing self-consciousness.

e. Edification means laying hold of people and putting them in service as stones in the building of the temple which in its totality is the body of Christ. The presupposition, of course, is that Christ is the foundation. A sermon does not have to be directed so much at knowing, willing, and feeling, but through these at our attitude so that an attitude of love may arise from faith, which sustains hope and carries with it the salt of repentance. The true point of preaching is thus the priestly mediation of the spiritual life.

When we look back at the previous definitions, a formal and structural comparison shows that Nitzsch's definition is much more fully developed than that of Hollaz, and that by a mediating concept he has related the two standpoints which Hollaz left unrelated. In distinction from Palmer's definition one might say that Nitzsch's is both externally and materially fuller than Palmer's definition, which has a rather ad hoc sound. Comparison with Schleiermacher also gives evidence first of the formal distinction that Nitzsch goes beyond Schleiermacher by introducing the nexus denoted by the terms Word of God, scripture, and church. This also involves historical and systematic comparison and classification. Nitzsch belongs to the category of mediating theologians. In two ways Nitzsch's theology of preaching brings to light the mediating character of his theological thinking.

First, he mediates in some sense between the positions of Hollaz and Schleiermacher. He does so by his central concept of the "witness," who is for him the convinced believing personality. There was a gap in the view of Hollaz at this point. Hollaz postulated correct explication and application in the preacher, but he did not answer the question: Who is capable of this? Nitzsch's answer is that it is the called witness, the regenerate personality, who can minister to the congregation with its legacy of faith and who is given the ability to mediate between God's Word and humanity.

If this side of the mediating thought of Nitzsch points to Schleiermacher, the other side points back from Schleiermacher to the theological tradition of the Reformation. Schleiermacher had almost completely eliminated the distinction between preacher and congregation, or between the congregation and what the preacher has to say to it. Nitzsch shows again that the subject matter of preaching, that which stands in need of explication and application, is different from humanity in the plight from which it has to be rescued. He brings to light again the whence and the whither of proclamation in their distinctiveness, but at the same time—following Schleiermacher here rather than diverging from him—he also answers the question as to the way that can and must be taken from the whence to the whither. The answer that Nitzsch offers is suggested already by the concept of the called witness in the sphere of the church.

Nitzsch again goes beyond Schleiermacher inasmuch as words like church and holy scripture are significant for him. Developing the legacy of Schleiermacher, he has enriched it. He has also clarified the questions raised by it. In contrast to Schleiermacher's distinctive vocabulary, to a large extent he has rediscovered the vocabulary of the Bible and the Reformation. As a result, he unavoidably comes up against certain problems arising out of the terminology and form of the older theology. He feels the problem of history more sharply, looking back on the one hand as terms like church and holy scripture take on importance, looking ahead on the other hand as theology focuses more concretely on the contemporary situation. The problem of the sermon as that of the encounter between God's Word on the one side and human being on the other comes into view again in Nitzsch, and hence he does at least give some indication of a new understanding of the task as distinct from Schleiermacher. One has to emphasize, however, that there has not been any real development and enrichment of Schleiermacher. The concept of the witness along with its more precise definition, which was meant to be an answer to the question as to the possibility of preaching, does not really take us beyond Schleiermacher's approach. At this central point there is no trace of an adoption of the Reformation tradition.

Thus the question that we must put to Nitzsch concerns this central concept of the called witness. Nitzsch offers three more precise definitions. Three things make the preacher the called witness.

1. The first is the ability to engage in correct explication. The Word of God is communicated only in scripture. The preacher has to lift it out of scripture and

present it in its true sense. To the question: How is it possible for a preacher to achieve authentic and objective explication of this kind? Nitzsch answers that the preacher has this ability as a cleansed, believing, born-again personality. Existence as such makes the preacher a sound expositor. It places God's Word in his hand and conscience, but without crushing him, without calling himself or his preaching into question.

2. Second, the called witness has the task of preaching in a living relationship to the existing situation. The demand that he imitate the divine condescension and recognize and heal real human conditions, linking a true knowledge of humanity with a knowledge of social, economic, and political relations, is binding on the preacher. If this demand, too, gives rise to the question: Who, then, can preach?, the answer lies once again in a reference to existence as a believing and regenerate personality. This is what enables the preacher to meet the demand.

3. The third constitutive factor arises out of a consideration of the goal or result of the sermon. This is described as the edification of the congregation of the Lord. Nitzsch fills out this concept from the New Testament. As he sees, it, it is a grasping of people. They are put in service and used. Indeed, they are assimilated to Christ as manifested in the development of an attitude of love deriving from faith. To create and mediate a self-consciousness as thus defined is the true task of preaching.

Precisely in relation to this comprehensive Christological development of the concept of edification, however, the answer to the question of the subject of the sermon that can and should effect this edification, namely, the reference once again to vital regenerate personality, gives us good reason to question any such confidence on material grounds. We have to ask whether the foundation, i.e., the preacher as a cleansed and believing personality, can carry the structure that is to be built upon it, from correct explication and application to an edifying of the congregation that is equivalent to assimilation to Christ. Or do we have here the assurance with which the people of the late-eighteenth and nineteenth centuries sought to intervene in what takes place between God and us, thus making an illegitimate claim? If the term "called" and the placing of the witness in the sphere of the church might have helped us understand the phrase "called witness" in relation to the church (in which the Holy Spirit bears witness to himself by calling people in it and making them hear and speak), Nitzsch's more precise interpretation of the word "called" in the three points just mentioned rules out this understanding.

Nor does anything else that he says point in this direction. Nitzsch defines the subject of proclamation as the Word of God transmitted through the texts of holy scripture. When scripture transmits God's Word to the preacher, this obviously means that scripture is not itself God's Word as such. It is a medium, an envelope. But if the expositor is to be able to differentiate between the form and matter of its contents, the *proprium* and the *accidens,* he must have a criterion by which to find God's Word in scripture. This being so, however, the expositor is no longer in the strict sense a hearer of scripture, but is on the same level as the scriptural witness, a colleague. The possibility of reproducing God's Word is the critical criterion for the expositor. Therefore, even though mediacy is stressed in the tie to scripture, the implication is unavoidable that a human being can have God's Word, even if indirectly. The question is: Can we humans trust ourselves, even indirectly, to know God's Word directly, and ascribe to ourselves collegiality with the scriptural witness?

Even the statement that the meaning and goal of proclamation is edification, quite apart from the idea that the preacher can supposedly accomplish this unaided, raises problems when edification is understood as a renewal of the self-consciousness that encompasses knowledge, will, and feeling, as the birth of a new attitude. The goal and result of the sermon achieve concreteness for Nitzsch in a psychological statement. Yet he also offers a more precise biblical definition of the term "attitude" along the line of faith, hope, and love. Even so the question arises: Why does not Nitzsch simply stay with faith as the result of proclamation? Why does he have to find its climax in a psychological concept? When we say "faith" we certainly cannot ignore the psychological side of this reality, let alone deny it. As it is human beings that believe, we can undoubtedly make psychological statements about faith. But in so doing we say nothing about the real essence of faith. Faith is essentially *God's* relation to us and ours to *God.* This relation owes its force and reality to its starting point and finishing point. It is what it is only on this basis. Faith does not exist apart from its constant relational character.

Nitzsch made a fatal mistake when he used attitude instead of faith. He wants to say something concrete and palpable. But the fact that attitude can be used abstractly shows clearly that what is meant is something other than what the New Testament means by *pistis* (faith). For the most part, of course, attitude does have an object. It too, then, is a relation. But it may also be without an object. It may be real and meaningful in itself. In the case of faith, however, there is no such "also." The change of concept in Nitzsch raises the question: Is it really the task of preaching to give rise to an attitude? If so, is success worth the cost that this is what is meant by the words church, holy scripture, correct exposition, and edification, i.e., assimilation to Christ? Can the attitude that is sought really be described as new? And if attitude is supposedly identical to faith, by which alone God justifies the sinner, the precipice of work-righteousness is not avoided.

The concept of a Christian personality which can know the Word of God and know and edify humanity, and the concept of a proclamation whose goal and result in us is a new human attitude, give rise to problems which warn us not be content with the answer that Nitzsch offers to the question of preaching but to inquire further.

6. JOHANNES BAUER

The next theory of preaching that we shall discuss, that of Johannes Bauer, brings us closer to our own day. In the meantime Albrecht Ritschl had come on the scene. With his concentration and reduction of the problem of theology to that of ethics, Ritschl had reached back beyond Schleiermacher to the Enlightenment. He was followed by E. Troeltsch and the history-of-religions school, which was in part a reaction to Ritschl inasmuch as it found a place not only for the ethical but also for the non-ethical, i.e., the irrational and the experiential. In this regard it was closer to Schleiermacher. It also brought with it a deepening of Ritschlian systematics.

In the first edition of the encyclopedia *Die Religion in Geschichte und Gegenwart,* the Heidelberg theologian Johannes Bauer, in the article "Homiletik," advocated a doctrine of preaching which in its systematic and fundamental defectiveness is characteristic of the theology that dominated the years leading up to the war [World War I]. We have here a theology that is totally superficial, verbose, ill-defined, and in the final analysis obscure. Systematic clarity and unambiguity were simply not to be had at that time. An attempt was usually made to replace them by the reference to some kind of individual depth of soul, to personality, or to experiences, which would all in some way indicate what was needed.

It is difficult, then, to find a definition of preaching in Bauer. He describes it in one place as the "free, individual, living confession of faith in personal proclamation of saving faith." Its aim is the "determining of the will of the listener to make a decision for a specific religious and ethical concept, experience, or act." Its effectiveness depends on "the personal conviction of the preacher concerning the truth of what he espouses, the gospel." The "best apologetic preaching" is the "simple, convinced, and enthusiastic presentation of the life of faith itself." The criteria of preaching are as follows: Does it promote a devout Christian life, winning as many as possible, and if possible not repelling any? Above all, does it correspond to the individuality of the preacher, thus being authentic? A biblical text is recommended for the sermon, because it is necessary that the Bible should be expounded to the congregation, and because the Bible is a common authority for preacher and congregation to which the preacher can appeal if the need arises. Furthermore, the preacher will find sure testimony and fruitful thoughts in the Bible. At the same time, Bauer does not rule out the sermon without a text. He then refers also to the problems that modern historical criticism has caused for preachers. But preachers have much to thank this for, e.g., a more vital understanding of the prophets and the historical Jesus.

We at once recognize here a disastrous regression as compared to Nitzsch, in whom the explication and application of the biblical text were differentiated and related, and a very instructive and living problematic emerged. Bauer, however, shows neither urgency nor sharpness in facing up to the demands of a doctrine of preaching. The individuality of the preacher is advanced unchecked as the leading principle. That this not be violated is the main homiletical concern. Wherever we look, whether it be at the discussion of the nature of preaching, its goal, its effect, its criteria, its relation to the text, everywhere it is the preacher that is to be free, alive, individual, personal, convinced, and enthusiastic. The preacher is the center, the foundation on which everything is to be built.

Naturally, behind this rampant subjectivism there is something objective, though it is, of course, hard to determine. Bauer talks about the gospel, about the matter itself, about saving faith. The objective side, however, is not to be determined from the biblical text. The text is merely desirable. It is not an integrating element in the actual concept of preaching. Bauer handles the Bible more freely than all the other theologians, apart from Schleiermacher and Vinet, whom we have discussed thus far.

The one thing that is very clear in Bauer's doctrine of preaching is the very positively described purpose of the sermon. With astounding confidence ministers are given full authority to show from their own life of faith what is good for their hearers, what these ought to experience, think, and desire, and to bring this about. Is this not an incredible claim? Where do preachers get authorization for it? The most concrete point in Bauer's doctrine of preaching is also the most questionable.

The criteria of preaching here are whether a sermon attracts or repels, whether it promotes a devout life, and whether it is authentic and in keeping with the pastor's individuality. Authenticity and a devout life are prerequisites, and preaching is an action between authentic preacher and devout listener. Should the preacher be liberal and the listener pietistic or orthodox, it is the sacred task of preaching to bridge the antitheses. The fact that such a gross consideration should be the climax of a doctrine of preaching is the sign of a sick and sorry situation with a very serious background: the plight of the church that has totally forgotten its task, the plight of ministers who are put in congregations with this meager understanding, and the plight of their defrauded congregations.

7. KARL FEZER

We now move on to discuss the doctrine of preaching advanced by Karl Fezer, Professor of Practical Theology at Tübingen. He has left us two definitions on preaching. The first may be found in his book *Das Wort Gottes und die Predigt* (1925): "Preaching is a cooperative human effort to bring it about by free speech that the God who has given us his fellowship in the Word of scripture is commonly present to a circle of others by the Holy Spirit."

The second definition is found in the second edition of *Die Religion in Geschichte und Gegenwart,* in the article "Predigt" (1930): "Preaching is the ministry, commanded to the church, of passing on to contemporaries the witness to revelation that is entrusted to it in scripture, in obedience to the God who acts with us in this word of scripture and in faith that this God in his grace and faithfulness, in, with, and under its poor human word, will himself be present among us as the living God, and will use our human word to speak his own Word."

We see at once here a definite advance on the positions of all the theologians discussed thus far. In particular, the superiority of the preacher is abandoned in the first definition. The preacher is no longer the one who leads, who gives, who mediates. The preacher steps back. God is the subject of the decisive process. It is he who edifies and gives, not the preacher, whose only concern is to cooperate. It is not just that an enlightened witness is now talking; instead, someone is at work.

At the heart of the entire definition stands the pow-

erful statement about the God who grants us his fellowship. There is a pointer here to the atonement, to
Christ. God as Son gives us what we need. He gives us
himself in the work of scripture. God and scripture, the
material and formal principles, no longer stand abstractly alongside one another. They are meaningfully
combined. Already in the concept of preaching the
combination comes with scripture. The concern of
preaching is solely with God himself, who gives himself to us in scripture, from election to redemption. He
himself is at work in us by the Holy Spirit. Thus the
problem of the hearer is also solved. God creates the
hearing congregation by the Holy Spirit. In it there
takes place a human effort whose aim is that God himself will act and be present. In this divine act human
speech merely assists. The instrument is free speech.
Here is the weakest point in the whole definition. But
we can hardly charge Fezer with this relic of liberalism
since he himself corrected it in a second definition.

In this second definition we note a further move
away from the subjective sphere. Human effort has
disappeared. It has been replaced by the ministry which
the church is commanded to render. The preacher is no
longer the subject; the church is now the subject as
God's instrument. Ministry means the rejection of all
sovereignty of preaching. Naturally, preaching is a
human effort, a human work. Its only basis, however,
lies in the command of God. The church is not a society
that itself sets up its cultus and preaching. It must be
obedient to a command.

What the preacher has to do is no longer denoted by
the misleading and meaningless term "free speech."
His task is to pass on the witness to revelation that is
entrusted to the church in scripture. It is a matter, then,
not of immediacy, but of mediacy and communication,
which is possible because God in his grace has en-

trusted scripture to the church with the duty of passing it on.

The idea of cooperation, which could be taken synergistically, has now been dropped. The new and fuller expression that replaces it clearly expresses the difference in levels between God's work and ours. We are not God's colleagues. Our work is done in obedience and in faith that God will use our human word, expressly called poor, to speak his own Word in or in spite of it.

The word must be directed to contemporaries. The focus here is on the need that sermons should be relevant and up to date. They must have the character of address and hit home to people and claim them in their concrete situations.

Undoubtedly we have here what is both systematically and fundamentally the most outstanding theory of preaching thus far. Nevertheless, even here we have some further questions to put which we may divide into two groups: (a) Questions or objections relating to specific thoughts and terms; and (b) Questions directed more comprehensively at the definition as a whole.

a. In the first group we ask:

i. What does Fezer mean by passing on the entrusted witness to revelation? Could not this be taken to mean that the church has something in its hand that it may use at its own discretion? Is there not here too strong an emphasis on subjective possession? In fact, the church has nothing in its hands, not even the possibility of passing on. What we must ask, then, is that it should be made clear in the definition that even the word of scripture is witness to God only insofar as it is evaluated as such.

ii. Then there is the question of the relation between the sermon and the text. The definition speaks of passing on the witness to revelation that is entrusted to the church in scripture. In a sermon, however, one does not pass on scripture as a whole but only a specific verse or passage. Ought not this to have been mentioned in the definition to obviate the suspicion that Fezer is thinking of free speech that is not based on a specific text but is simply in accord with the content of revelation in general, i.e., preaching on a theme? In fact, Fezer does not recognize sermons without texts. The possibility of a misunderstanding of that kind must be blamed on the need for brevity. Again, even though formally a sermon may deal with only a small part of scripture, materially it does in fact present the whole.

iii. In this connection we must also ask whether the relation between preaching and the church's other activities in the educational and pastoral fields has received careful enough consideration. Do not all the church's activities fall under the definition, so that what distinguishes preaching is missing? In fact, however, preaching cannot be differentiated from education and pastoral care. The essence of the church is proclamation. What we have are merely variations on the one task.

iv. A further question is whether the idea of contemporaries is the right one. In a strictly theological definition, ought we not to understand those who are addressed theologically? Contemporaries are really listeners only when God makes them such, i.e., when they are in the church. The concern of preaching is with the human existence which God has accepted, to which he has given his Spirit, so that every today is a qualified today. A circuit is set up. God speaks and causes his Word to penetrate the hearts of the listeners by the Holy Spirit. The objection we raise is a valid one. The only danger is that at first the circuit is still broken. Fully aware of the danger of misunderstanding, we may thus let the idea of contemporaries stand so long as no opposition to "church" is intended.

v. It should be noted that the definition does not

mention the preacher. There is in some sense a gap there. Since, however, the person is not constitutive for the concept of preaching, there are good reasons for Fezer's omission. Materially the lacuna is of no significance.

b. In the second group:

i. Our first question relates to Fezer's statement that preaching *is* the ministry commanded to the church. Would it not be better to say that it comes to be, or ought to be, or is an attempt to be this ministry? "Is" can be said only when God is truly present. This means that unless God is truly present, preaching is not preaching. The idea of an attempt does not have to involve the danger of a lack of faith in God's promise.

ii. How does Fezer see the relation between God's Word and the human word? Is not the idea that preaching, too, needs justification stated very weakly and obscurely by his reference to our "poor human word"? Should it not be stressed instead that God is at work in spite of the human word, that the human word is always corrupt, that it is good only by the grace of God? That Fezer sees the problem is shown by his recognition that preaching as a human effort is always an impossible enterprise. The systematic problem is also hinted at in his idea of the "poor human word." Nevertheless, he does not see the matter as it is seen in the objection. Yet the focus should not be on the corrupt human action but on the command and the promise of God. Without weakening the truth of the objection, we are not to look back in preaching but to look ahead. In this connection we may refer to Luther's saying that the petition "Forgive us our debts" is not to be extended to preaching.

8. Leonhard Fendt

From Fendt we have the following definition: "Evangelical preaching is the form of Evangelical worship in which an academically trained Christian who has also been called by the congregation tries to present the Christian kerygma as we have it in the New Testament to the people of his own day in their own terms, but without impairing or supplementing the substance of the kerygma, and to do this, not for pedagogic, aesthetic, or other important human reasons, but because the Christian kerygma is the Word to which the promise is annexed that by this Word the Holy Spirit will awaken faith wherever and whenever God pleases."

Like Fezer's definition, this definition of Leonhard Fendt differs from that of Bauer inasmuch as it stands on the basis of a theology that takes God seriously. But it has some distinctive features. Three points in particular call for notice.

a. The definition speaks of the substance of the Christian kerygma "as we have it in the New Testament." For Fendt, however, the heart of the Christian kerygma is that Jesus of Nazareth is the Christ of God for us. The substance of the kerygma is thus a sharply definable concept which is seen as the specific point of the New Testament but from which the Old Testament is excluded.

b. Fendt defines it as the preacher's duty to present the kerygma to "the people of his own day," which means that he must form and shape it in such a way that his contemporaries can understand and appropriate it.

c. The statement that "the Christian kerygma is the Word to which the promise is annexed" means that a definable Word is identified as the Christian kerygma as thus understood.

Three additional features of the definition are less significant.

d. By defining preaching as a form of worship, Fendt obviously intends to distinguish and demarcate it from teaching.

e. He qualifies the preacher in some sense by saying that he must be an academically trained and eloquent Christian.

f. The phrase "not for pedagogic, aesthetic, or other important human reasons" carries an express polemic against the misdirection and misuse of the church's proclamation.

Having now concluded our discussion of definitions of preaching, we gather from it that a definition of preaching will have nine constitutive elements:

1. Revelation or the Word of God
2. The church as the place of preaching
3. The divine command
4. The special ministry of the preacher
5. The thought of preaching as an attempt
6. The relation to scripture
7. The concept of individual speech
8. The concept of the congregation
9. The Holy Spirit as the starting point, center, and conclusion

Offense might be taken at the strictly human procedure of regarding these nine elements as constitutive for the concept of preaching. Why just nine? Why not more? Why not fewer? Does not the church have something basic and authoritative to say on the matter? Nevertheless, the church, too, can only look outside itself to the gospel that underlies it and to the dogmas that establish its teaching. It is then the business and duty of theologians to reflect seriously on the mission and doctrine of the church on the basis of the biblical

documents. But these reflections, which come to expression in doctrinal views and the most varied theolo-
gies, are very far from being dogma. They can never be
more than dogmatic statements and have to be evaluated as such. This is why we do not have a common
Protestant theology. We do not have a consensus. We
do not have authoritative church direction to serve as
a guideline for professors and pastors. A visible and
tenable consensus is something that Protestantism
completely lacks.

II. An Attempt at a New Definition

1. *"Preaching is the Word of God which he himself speaks,
claiming for the purpose the exposition of a biblical text in free
human words that are relevant to contemporaries by those who are
called to do this in the church that is obedient to its commission."*

2. *"Preaching is the attempt enjoined upon the church to serve
God's own Word, through one who is called thereto, by expounding
a biblical text in human words and making it relevant to contemporaries in intimation of what they have to hear from God himself."*

Externally these two formulas contain all that we
have come up with thus far. The same elements occur
in both, each in its own place, each seen from the decisive standpoint. Together they form the answer to the
question of the relation between the Word of God and
the human word.

The totality forms a closed circle which begins with
God and ends with him.

The difference in approaches—first from the top
down, then from the bottom up—is grounded in the
fact that one cannot answer the question of preaching
in a single statement. The answer lies beyond what can
be said in a single answer. If we want to speak honestly

and conscientiously about the true reality, we can only set up a signpost that points past human reflection to *the* subject that lives and moves in itself, that remains the subject and never becomes the content of a concept.

Behind the two formulas there finally stands the decisive statement of Christology regarding the unity between God and us in Jesus Christ. The difficulty of preaching is none other than that of trying to say who and what Jesus Christ is. Theologians must go both ways, the way of descending and the way of ascending thought. This means, however, that they can seek to be only signposts, pointing fingers. Only brokenly and very imperfectly can they discharge their mission as proclaimers of God's Word.

Their speech is "free" speech in the sense that it is their own. It does not consist of reading or exegesis. They speak the scriptural word that they have heard, as their own independent word. The task of preachers is like that of the apostles, though on a different level. In a limited sense they, too, have a "prophetic office." For this they must at any rate have *exousia* (authority).

If we ask whether a synthesis of the two formulas is possible on the basis of Christ, in whom is achieved the unity of the Old and New Testaments, our only answer can be that all pagan religions reach out for this kind of synthesis, but Christian theology knows how to steer clear of any such attempt because it is the theology of the religion of revelation, and because a synthesis of this kind would mean an attack on the honor of God. Two things call for emphasis. First, God is the one who works, and second, we humans must try to point to what is said in scripture. There is no third thing.

This service that preachers must render the church, like theology in general, is only an attempt, for from our standpoint all that is possible is an attempt to serve the Word of God, to announce it, and to this extent it is an attempt that is commanded. The word "announcement" has the advantage over "proclamation" that in it God is the one who makes himself heard, who speaks, and not we, who simply have the role of announcing what God himself wants to say. This is what *epangelia* signifies in the New Testament. The word "announcement" does not really carry with it a summons to human decision. A decision of this kind, which is taken solely between God and us, is in no sense constitutive for the task of preaching. Preaching is an attempt which the church is ordered to make. For this reason the definition needs no more precise qualification of preaching than the emphasis that it should not merely be preaching but church preaching.

The concept of preaching cannot be fixed on the basis of experiences. It is a theological concept which arises in the faith that can only point to the divine reality.

2
Criteria of the Sermon

I. Revelation

Preaching must conform to revelation. First, this means negatively that in preaching we are not to repeat or transmit the revelation of God by what we do. Precisely because the point of the event of preaching is God's own speaking *(Deus loquitur),* there can be no question of our doing the revealing in any way. In all circumstances we must respect the fact that God *has* revealed himself and he will reveal himself as the one who comes again. All the action that takes place in preaching, which lies between the first advent and the second, is the action of the divine Subject. Revelation is a closed circuit in which God is both Subject and Object and the link between the two.

From this truth we may derive a few practical conclusions.

1. Preaching cannot try to be a proof of the truth of God. It cannot set out to prove God by an intellectual demonstration, by stating and stressing certain propositions. There can be no other proof of God than that which God himself offers.

Nor can it be the task of preaching to expound or present the truth of God aesthetically in the form of a picture, an impression, or an aesthetic evocation of

Jesus Christ. When Paul in Galatians 3:1 speaks of dis-
playing Christ before the eyes, it is the apostle speaking. But *we* stand under the commandment not to make
any images. If God himself wills to speak his truth,
preachers are forbidden to interfere with any science or
art of their own. In this light not only artistic represen-
tation of Christ and crucifixes in churches are questionable, but also the constructing of mental images of God.

2. Again, preaching may not try to create the reality
of God. Reference might be made to slogans which
imply a progression from mere word to reality, from
doctrine to life. Preaching, it is said, has the task of
building up the kingdom of God, of converting, of
leading to decision. It must confront us with the reality
of God. It must be vital and communicate an experience. It must bring to light our situation and set us
before God. Even though this situation be viewed with
Kierkegaard as one of sickness unto death, however,
this is too much to ask.

All these things may well happen in a sermon, of
course, but they are acts which God himself wills to
perform and which can never, therefore, be a human
task. If it is objected that we must be converted *in faith,*
i.e., in an awareness that what takes place is Christ's
doing, it can only be said that faith means looking to
Christ, so that the congregation is not left with the
impression that the preacher has a corner on Christ and
the Spirit. The insight that God is not a *Deus otiosus*
(inactive God) but an active God, and that we must
simply be obedient to our commission, but not engaged
in an action of our own choosing, imposes upon us a
demand for discipline.

Our preaching today differs from that of the prophets and apostles who saw and touched Christ. To be
sure, it does not differ qualitatively, but it differs inasmuch as it is done in a different place. If, however,
God speaks through our word, then the prophets and

apostles are actually there even though it be a simple pastor that speaks. Yet we should not be self-conscious about this, nor listen for our own prophetic booming, for even though Christ be present, it is by God's own action. Preachers are under a constraint, an *ananke* (1 Cor. 9:16) that strips them of all their own proposals and programs.

This being so, there is no place at all for the *scopus* of a sermon, whether theoretical (a formal theme or impressive proposition) or practical (the aim of directing listeners to a certain type of conduct). Preachers' plans of this kind can be nothing more than attempts to anticipate what God himself wills to do in the sermon. There will, of course, be a theme. Something will be presented *(tithetai)*. A statement will be made. But in the strictest sense it will be God's statement. In preaching God himself presents what he wills to present, and will present. If preachers think they should present a theme of their own, it will anticipate what God himself wants to say. If they offer their congregation a clever conceptual picture, even though it be arrived at by serious and intensive exegesis, it will not be scripture itself that speaks, but something will merely be said *about* scripture.

Second, and positively, preaching must be exposition of holy scripture. I have not to talk *about* scripture but *from* it. I have not to say something, but merely repeat something. If God alone wants to speak in a sermon, neither theme nor *scopus* should get in the way. If later there seems to be a clear-cut title, I must ask suspiciously whether I have not been following my own conceptual image or trying to achieve a unity that God alone can bring here. Our task is simply to follow the distinctive movement of thought in the text, to stay with this, and not with a plan that arises out of it.

Even in picking a text the same thing may happen as in picking a theme. I may reach into the Bible, find

something "nice," and lift it out. It is dangerous even
to address a specific congregational situation or experience in terms of a specific text. In such situations we
must bring the Bible as a whole to bear. Then God
might perhaps legitimately speak to the situation and
work a miracle. But we may not count on this. The
pastor might easily become the pope of his congregation, presenting his own idea instead of God's Word.

But we are considering the positive side of what it
means that preaching must conform to revelation. Our
initial point is that God himself wills to reveal himself.
He himself wills to attest his revelation. He himself—
not we—has done this and wills to do it. Preaching,
then, takes place in listening to the self-revealing will
of God. Preachers are drawn into this event. It is of
concern to them. They are called by this event. The
event becomes a constituent part of their own existence. Because God has revealed himself and wills to
reveal himself, and because preachers are confronted
by this event, their preaching—if they are commissioned to preach—is necessarily governed by it in both
content and form, in the logical content of what is said
and in their relation to the fact that God has revealed
himself and will reveal himself. Preaching is not a neu-
tral activity. It is not an action involving two equal
partners. It can mean only Lordship on God's side and
obedience on ours.

Only as preaching is controlled by this relation can
it be viewed as *kērygma,* i.e., as a message that a herald
is commissioned to deliver. When it is this the preacher
has full authority. But this authority rests on the authority of him who sends the herald. Being a *kēryx,* a
herald, means coming from the epiphany of Christ and
going toward the day of the Lord. It is in the double
movement, namely, that God *has* revealed himself and
will reveal himself, that preaching conforms to revelation in the New Testament sense.

The positive definition, too, has certain practical implications.

1. There is an unconditional "whence." God *has* revealed himself, the Word became flesh. God has assumed human nature. Humanity has become God's in Christ. In Christ God has made fallen humanity his own. Faced with the fall, God did not step angrily aside. Instead he has personally united himself with the race. Lost humanity has been called home.

This means that God *has* revealed himself. The last word of this incarnation was spoken in Christ's death. In Christ our guilt and punishment was lifted from us and taken away. In Christ we were reconciled to God— *eph' hapax* [Heb. 10:10], once and for all. Believing means seeing that this is so, that God has reconciled himself to us in Christ.

If preaching is to be governed by this "whence," then it can take place in no other attitude than that of the recipient; it can seek no other posture. It can be undertaken only in the knowledge that God himself has put everything right. Over against all doubt and contradiction, the truth is that the Word became flesh. All that was required has actually been done to meet all human need.

Preaching, however, has not only to say this. It is itself an event in face of the revelation that has taken place. It must set itself unconditionally under this presupposition. No matter what may be said in detail, this is the point from which every single line must be drawn. Not the mere word "Christ," not a mere description of Christ, but solely what God has done with us in Christ, Immanuel, God with us—this is the central point of all preaching.

What are we to regard as a word which in all circumstances meets this condition? Preachers are constantly tempted to proclaim human sins instead of this event, instead of God's goodness. Or heresy becomes the secret theme as, conscious of the correctness of their own views, they attack what they regard as mistaken opinions. Now certainly something has to be said about human sins and errors. Yet it ought to be said from the standpoint of sin forgiven and error removed. Sin undoubtedly has to be taken seriously, but forgiveness even more seriously. For either forgiveness is the first word or it is not true at all. Sin must be spoken about only as the sin which is taken away by the Lamb of God. Christian preaching deals with sin as *forgiven* sin. And as with sin, so also with the law. The law can be good only when it stands in relation to the gospel. We can certainly speak about the goodness of God. Because it is God's goodness, its light shines into human life. But abstract preaching about law is in no circumstances Christian preaching. The church can preach only the law that is set in relation to the gospel. It can speak about the commandment only with the injunction to fear God and to love him.

Along similar lines it is possible to insist on sanctification. If it is true that we are reconciled to God, how can this fail to involve a claim on humanity? How can we proclaim the gospel without listening to the law? But the reference to sanctification, like that to sin and the law, can be made only in the light of the unconditional "whence." The danger of preaching sin, law, and sanctification is greater in Calvinist preaching than in Lutheran. We will come back later to the danger in Lutheran preaching.

From first to last, figuratively speaking, a sermon must have a thrust. But this does not lie in the enthusiasm, faith, earnestness, or conviction of the preacher. The sermon takes on its thrust when it begins: "The Word became flesh *eph' hapax,* once and for all," and when account of this is taken in every thought. How many parts of sermons, especially so-called introductions, which are for the purpose of getting the attention

of the listeners, would be better left unspoken from
this standpoint. The real need is not so much to get to
the people as to come from Christ. Then one automatically gets to the people. Nothing should be said on any
other level than that of the Word made flesh. No position need be taken vis-à-vis the gospel. The preacher
should simply believe the gospel and say all he has to
say on the basis of this belief. This means that the
thrust of the sermon is always downhill, not uphill to
a goal. Everything has already taken place. (Even the
epistle to the Romans is not striving toward a goal.
Before Paul speaks about judgment, he writes 1:16f.,
and if we read chapters 1 and 2 aright, we see that 1:16f.
is the light that shines over the whole passage. Standing
under this sign, then, 1 and 2 are also the preaching of
grace.)

2. Second, we must speak about the unconditional
"whither" of preaching. This "whither" can be understood only when we recognize that the revelation, the
reconciliation, the fulfillment of Immanuel, God with
us, which, as the New Testament tells us, have taken
place unconditionally and once-for-all, are to be presented no less unconditionally as ahead of us in Jesus
Christ: yesterday, today, and forever. From first to last
the New Testament refers to the future of salvation. In
the New Testament, however, this does not in any way
contradict the *eph' hapax.* This once-for-all event is at
one and the same time both the whence of believers
and their whither. The New Testament which proclaims the Christ who has already come proclaims him
also as the Christ who one day will come. This day of
the appearing of Jesus Christ gives us orientation for
our life in faith, in Christ. It gives Christians their
whither no less unconditionally than their whence. The
two are the same: Jesus Christ, yesterday, today, and
forever. The awaiting of all things from Christ is eschatology. Hence Christian eschatology is none other

than Christology. If, then, revelation is ahead of preaching as well as behind it, the previously described attitude of receptivity, of gratitude and assurance, is also the attitude and movement of expectation. The expectation is that what has taken place already will take place again, that what has been given already will be given again. Preaching stands between the first advent and the second. So does the whole life of the Christian. Everything depends on our not falling victim to the whence alone, as if coming from the grace of God, as if Christian assurance meant a rest, a possessing, a final security. This assurance is in fact a profound nonpossessing. This wealth, as we turn to the future, is total poverty and lack. But it is also expectation and hope, the prospect of what will then be given us.

The Christian life is a striding from the one pole to the other, from having to not having, then to a confident reaching out for new riches. We walk by faith, not by sight (2 Cor. 5:7). Had we sight already, there would be neither a first advent nor a second, no yesterday, today, or tomorrow. But we walk by faith, i.e., in a double movement from Christ to Christ. Preaching must be a presentation of this walk by faith and not by sight. The assurance, the confidence, is not Christian assurance or confidence unless it is shot through with yearning for future salvation, for Christ, whom we constantly need afresh. Like the Christ who has appeared already, the Christ who is still to come must be the center of every sermon. All that we say must be subordinate to this: Christ comes, we await his day.

"The Word became flesh" can be spoken legitimately only when there follows at once: "Amen, come, Lord Jesus." Lutheran preaching has always had the charisma (gift) of understanding especially well the statement *ho logos sarx egeneto* (the Word became flesh). The danger, however, is that of overconfident insistence on the event that lies behind us. The result is dogmatic and experiential preaching. Philippians 2, however, is followed by Philippians 3: "Not that I have already attained, but I press on." This is how movement finally comes to rest. All preaching must have the total assurance of "It has happened, it is done" and also the forward thrust. It must stand under the insight that all things must change. We await a new heaven and a new earth. Indeed, we who are reconciled to God can be no more than guests in this life with the hope: "Lo, I make all things new." Christian preaching then, must be unconditionally the preaching of hope. Just because we speak about that which unconditionally is, we also speak unconditionally about that which will come to be. We may not stop at either the being or the becoming. But the step from the being to the becoming must be brought into view. The turn from yesterday to tomorrow is the meaning of the Christian "today." Hence preaching that conforms to revelation must be a race in the sense of Philippians 3. Preachers who set out from a fixed starting point are the very ones who must press on, who must hunger and thirst, though always with the promise that they will be satisfied. The homiletic art is to speak about the present, about experience, about the new life that has appeared in history, but it may not do so except with a thrust toward tomorrow. We are a people that walk in darkness. But we have seen a great light.

The two points that determine whether a sermon is in accord with revelation are Christmas and the day of Christ. If preaching is within these two points, it conforms to revelation. All that is said must always be said between these two points.

II. Church

Preaching must be done in the sphere of the church, i.e., in concrete connection with the existence and mission of the church.

When we speak about revelation in the Old and New Testaments, we do not refer to a general reality that takes place always and everywhere but to a specific, concrete, definite event at a specific time. Nor do we refer to a reality which might be achieved by human resources but to an event that happens to us, that is given to us. As regards the conformity of preaching to revelation, the result is that this is not a quality deriving from the condition of human existence, whether natural or historical. It is not a quality that bears any relation to a philosophy or worldview. It relates solely to the event which differs from all the events that we experience as one that is specifically given again and again. From another angle the relation between preaching and revelation cannot be seen as a feature that can be conferred or produced by any technique. It does not lie in our hands to initiate that movement from the first advent to the second. But when it really happens that preaching conforms to revelation, it is nothing but grace, it is solely the work of God.

When the double warning is heeded that the conformity of preaching to revelation cannot be defined in terms of any philosophy and is not a feature that we can confer, we can only consider that what we have here is a specific event that is given to us by grace. Aware of our impotence regarding it, we see that we are directed to a place which we have not first to discover, which we have not to select from any philosophical, political, or aesthetic standpoint, but into which we are simply forced, since it is the only place at which we can stand. This place is the church.

In this place we have a commitment that differs from any other commitment on earth, whether it be family, station, people, or race. This commitment is one that we see to be absolutely different from all created ties, for it means *en Christō einai* (being in Christ). Here in the church, where the word of reconciliation is pronounced, all those other ties are exposed and judged by the Word as unclean, poisoned, immersed in the sphere of the fall. But by the same word we also hear that every hurt is healed and that the whole burden of sinful ties is taken from us. Those who hear the Word of the God who is gracious to us then see that they are also his creatures, for the message of reconciliation, which the church is primarily to proclaim, also contains the message of creation. Where the Word of reconciliation creates human hearers for itself, there is the church, the *kyriakē ekklēsia*, the congregation of those whom the Lord has called. Only in this place where we are set by revelation can there be legitimate preaching, nor will this be on the basis of reflection on humanity, on the situation of the natural and historical cosmos, or the like. Only because the call of revelation goes out and people hear it does the church come into being. In preaching, conformity to the church follows conformity to revelation. Because preaching is done in this unique place to which the Word of the twofold advent comes and in which we are set with no cooperation on our part, preaching conforms to revelation for no reason that we can give.

Two points must be made in elucidation. Article VII of the Augsburg Confession describes the true church as follows: *evangelium pure docetur et recte administrantur sacramenta* (the gospel is purely taught and the sacraments are rightly administered). By bringing the sacraments and the preaching of the gospel together, the article shows us what is the link between being put in a specific place and the conformity of preaching to revelation. Significantly, we put the sacraments first, for we do not know what preaching is if we have no knowledge of the sacraments. There is preaching in the full sense only where it is accompanied and explained by the sacraments. What happens in the sacraments is that with visible signs we are pointed to the event of revelation that underlies and is promised to the church, and this in a way which, unlike that of preaching and all else that the church does, is not just a matter of words but of visible, bodily action.

Baptism confirms church membership. Life begins with baptism, not with birth. The point of being baptized is that a relation is set up between revelation and the baptized in a specific place (Rom. 6:3). This *ebaptisthēmen eis Christon Iēsoun* (being baptized into Christ Jesus) does not merely involve a reference to the *eph' hapax* of revelation but, with and beyond all that can be said, it involves the event of *baptisma*. If baptism denotes the event of revelation from which we come, however, the Lord's Supper is a sign of the same event, but now understood as the coming event that is awaited by us (1 Cor. 11:26).

It is in this church in which are administered the sacrament of grace and the sacrament of hope—and both are both—that preaching takes place. Because both the sacraments and preaching can take place meaningfully only in the church, it is true of both that they are legitimate only in their relation to one another. Preaching as the specific event, the *signum* (sign), which can point us to the great Christian theme is legitimate only when it derives from that other *signum* which in the form of an event points to the event of revelation. It is legitimate, then, only when it does not seek to be anything other than a commentary, an interpretation of the sacraments, a reference to the same thing, but now in words. When the need is seen that preaching must be a *signum*, even a sacramental act—sacramental in the sense of distinct, defined, different from every other possibility—then we have good reason to place ourselves where this demand can be met, since it is there that God has promised us this grace. The place is the church. In the light of what God does in baptism and the Lord's Supper—that God himself elects us for membership of Christ's body and gives us food and drink for our pilgrimage to eternal life—in this light our preaching is done, namely, in the knowledge that all our listeners are baptized and thus called to a state of grace, and that what has taken place already will undoubtedly take place again. With the reference to baptism and the Lord's Supper, the demand that preaching have a backward and forward thrust, a whence and a whither, achieves concreteness, and we are given the place in which we must inwardly set ourselves as proclaimers of the Word.

If we now look at the real situation of the Protestant church in the light of these basic considerations, we immediately note at this point an obvious lacuna. At the Reformation the Roman church of the sacraments was replaced by the church of the Word on the basis of the gospel. But very soon this was taken to mean that the administration of the sacraments might be omitted from worship as nonessential, all the emphasis now being put on the sermon. Today, then, we have Rome on the one side, still the sacramental church, and Protestantism on the other, the preaching church, which also administers the sacraments, but not so publicly. Both the Roman Catholic and the Protestant overemphases represent a disruption, a distortion, and even a destruction of the church. What kind of preaching is it that receives its prominence from suppression of the sacraments, that cannot refer to the sacraments which it has to interpret and by which it is to be interpreted? We do not live by what our pastors can say but by the fact that we are baptized, that God has called us.

Today, it is true, everyone can see the lack and attempts are being made to make it good by all kinds of substitutes such as the renewing and deepening of the liturgy, the richer embellishment of worship with music, and similar devices. But all these efforts are doomed to failure in advance because they rest on a totally wrong orientation.

Appeal is wrongly made to Luther in these circles. Luther certainly wanted to take over as much as possible of the liturgical riches of the Roman Mass, but to include Communion. Calvin untiringly urged that Communion should be administered at every Sunday service. The weakness today is that we do not administer the sacraments at Sunday worship. In practice baptism ought to come at the beginning of the service—in the presence of the congregation—and Communion at the end. The sermon would then have its meaningful place in the middle between the two. Of a service of this kind it could then rightly be said: *recte administrare sacramenta et pure docere evangelium.* But so long as we do not grasp what Evangelical worship is in its entirety, our theological efforts, including the liturgical movement, will be invalid. Only when there is true worship with both sermon and sacrament can the liturgy be given its rightful place, for only then can it fulfill its purpose, namely, to lead up to the sacrament. In every respect the church is a physical, historical entity, with true and visible corporeality, and yet in every respect it is also wholly invisible as the mysterious body of Christ. Because the church is both at one and the same time, there must never in any circumstances be separation between the administration of the sacraments and the proclamation of the gospel.

We would surely be better Protestants if we would let Roman Catholicism with its onesidedness remind us of what we are missing. Precisely in order to be able to confront Roman Catholicism we need to know about the sacraments again. In the last resort the liturgical movement is simply an expression of the longing for the beautiful services of the Roman Catholic Church. But it is not liturgical enrichment that we should be seeking. We simply need to be told what it means that the sacraments are administered in the church. It would be a genuine anti-Roman Protestantism that would let itself be told this and yet still have a concern for real preaching.

Preaching can only be a human repetition referring us to the event of the preceding revelation. If we differentiate between the That of preaching and the What, the sacraments stand on the one side and scripture on the other. The sacraments are a pointer within the church's existence to the That of revelation, while scripture is a pointer to the quality of the event, to the What. But it is futile to set the sacraments and scripture over against one another, for ultimately they are different determinations of the same thing. The church is there when holy scripture is there as concrete witness to the concrete event of revelation. Revelation as a divine action takes place in the midst of human life and human history. In order that the event may be present and true for us, holy scripture is needed as witness. By it the prophets and apostles mediate revelation to us. The church is not immediate to revelation. It is built on the foundation of witnesses with an extraordinary call, the prophets in the Old Testament, and in the New Testament the *apostoloi,* who were called to be the apostles of the church. As witness to revelation is given in the church, the event of the church should show that it does not live for itself alone, that its life is not its own independent life, but that it is founded on the absolutely unique event of the divine action which took place in Israel and Christ. Israel and Christ are the focal points of revelation—a people and the Redeemer. On the one side is a straying, waiting, sinning people, yet a people not abandoned by God. On the other side is the fullness of grace, the Savior of the people, the fulfillment of the law, and therefore the gospel. Because revelation is not a general relation between God and the world, because it took place only *once,* we have to recognize the concreteness of holy scripture. The restriction to scripture is a sign of the singularity and uniqueness of revelation.

The church is not humanity in general in relation to God. It is humanity gathered around the one event. The church is the church that is based on *this* scripture. If this is the relation between the church and scripture, if the church is constituted by the testimony of the apostles, by revelation, what is then the task of preaching? It has simply to repeat the testimony by which the church is constituted. It has to be witness to that witness, to the revelation attested by holy scripture. We are thus brought up against the fact that the sermon must be a text sermon. Preaching has to be *biblical* preaching. As it relates to the sacraments, it relates also to the word of the prophets and apostles. We can give no reason for the uniqueness of the Bible, for the choice of this literature. We start out from the fact that the church is the place where the *Bible* is opened. Here God has spoken. Here he has given us a commission, a command. This is why we dare to do what has to be done. The church is a place where we *are* chosen by the voice of revelation. Scripture is before us, and preaching must follow with due attention to what is given there. We can emancipate ourselves from the Bible as little as children can from their duties to parents.

In the presence of the two facts of the sacraments and scripture, preaching must take place. The sacraments bear witness that the event has occurred, while scripture bears witness to the content of the event. The conformity of preaching to the church is guaranteed when it relates to the sacraments and scripture, when its poles, its sacramental character and its conformity to scripture, are secure. As a circle has both a center and a periphery, and neither is more important than the other, so both sermon and sacraments belong to worship in the full sense.

III. Confession*

In the foregoing deliberations we have emphasized that preaching must rest on command. It must be done in obedience to a commission. In this way it achieves conformity to confession. When the church undertakes to proclaim the Word of God, this is not because it seeks to fulfill a plan or to serve an abstract purpose. Even the best purpose can have no place in a definition of what the church is doing. The action related to fact is not to be derived from any principle. It is based on a commission, a command. Executing a plan or serving a purpose might come into consideration if it were just a matter of educating the race. The church might then involve itself deeply in human needs and educate people to be real people. But if we look at what has gone before and think of the true definition of the church and preaching, this is not the point. The church is not a tool to uphold the world or to further its progress. It is not an instrument to serve either what is old or what is new. The church and preaching are not ambulances on the battlefield of life. Preaching must not attempt to set up an ideal community, whether of soul or heart or spirit. Undoubtedly all these things are laudable. All are worth striving for. There has to be this kind of work. It may go along with preaching. Even linguisti-

---

*In the discussion that follows, Barth several times refers back to this heading as "Commission."—Trans.

cally these things have their place in preaching as in human life. None of us can evade them. Pastor and Christians are people. They live in the world. We must not overlook this. But the moment preaching makes these things its end, it becomes superfluous. This has become especially clear today. Other agencies have long since taken over cultural tasks. This being so, the church might abandon them and die as the church (a thought once presented by Richard Rothe when he spoke of the future absorption of the church into the state). Enough is being done for life, for the soul, and for the family by the media and politics. In matters of public morality and the like, the children of the world can do better. The church will simply be a fifth wheel. In the church it is essential that we remember the command, the commission. In the church we must have people who obey a constraint that is laid upon them from without, that is no less real than the fact of their birth and their death. The church can do no other than recognize that it has a command, and that this command must be obeyed. It will have a right to exist again when it understands its existence again, i.e., its existence on the basis of a call. It will then be the *ekklēsia* again. Preaching as a function of worship must be a declaration of the church's obedience to the task which Christ has given it by revelation. This is preaching as the *anankē* (constraint) to which Paul refers: "Woe is me if I do not preach the gospel!" Paul does not have a plan; he has a commission.

From all the above the following points emerge and demand consideration if our sermons are to be authentic sermons.

If it is true that preaching means obedience, calling, and commission, then it has to have a confessional character. But what is confession? Confession of faith cannot mean that we are expressing what lives in us, or that we are thinking certain things in common. *Professio fidei* (professing the faith) means stating what we believe, what we who say *credimus* (we believe) must believe and confess because we have been listening to revelation. Confession is response, making answer, to what has been said. Preaching cannot be done except according to the norm of the confessions that are recognized in the church. No sermon can be anything other than an act of response to the call, closely connected to the creed. What happens here does not happen according to a plan or on the basis of an idea. Here something is heeded. We have heard the Word of God and we answer with the confession, with the creed: *Credo,* I believe in the Father, the Son, and the Holy Spirit. Emphasis on the confession, however, should not mean preaching the confessions (the creeds, the Augsburg Confession, etc.). We are simply saying that preachers should pay attention to the familiar confessions of their churches as the goal and limit of what they say, in this way putting themselves in the place where the church stands.

A second practical implication relates to the question of edificatory preaching. What is to be edified? Obviously the church itself. But here edification is not to be understood as in the *Shepherd of Hermas,* where it has the sense of ongoing building, or building up, or integrating. The point is that the church must be built afresh each time. It must constitute itself. Its members must receive the command and be obedient. *"By* obedience *to* obedience" is the goal, and it is also the edifying of the church. In the church the congregation is built up as a fellowship, as a congregation standing under revelation and hearing the Word of God. Only within this framework may there also be the second aspect: edification to life by the grace of God. When this is noted, then education, aid, etc., have their place; the frontier is not drawn too closely. Little huts may be built in the shadow. Pastors may also talk about all these things.

They may act and work and play a part in culture. But all such things are to be only the zeros after the one. Conformity to the confession is the one. Nothing must be subtracted from this nor anything put before it. The first thing is this: "Seek first the kingdom of God" (Matt. 6:33); "One thing is necessary" (Luke 10:42).

IV. Ministry

The event of preaching consists of the fact that in the church, which as such has the commission to preach, individuals step forth from the ranks to give witness to the congregation concerning the redemption and the reconciliation to God that has taken place in Christ. The question of the legitimacy of this stepping forth arises along with the question of the conformity of preaching to ministry. Now if we disregard the apostolate, we have to state that the New Testament gives no special emphasis to the problem of the ministry. True, it makes occasional mention of the *episkopoi* and *presbyteroi* who were called by the apostles and recognized by the congregations. But we cannot derive from this any doctrine of the ministry.

In dealing with the question of the ministry we must not overlook the institution of the church and the apostles. The existence of the ministry is thus bound up with that of the church. According to Matthew 16:18f. (cf. 18:15–20), the church is at once instituted in a specific order: Peter representing the apostles, then the community in distinction from the apostolate. Simultaneously, then, the *una sancta ecclesia* (one holy church) is the *ecclesia docens* (teaching church) and the *ecclesia audiens* (hearing church). Wherever the church is, there also is correspondence to this order—not its repetition, for the institution of the apostles is a unique event—as certain people in succession to the apostles have to do again what they did for the first time. To the extent that the church is the body of Christ, the preacher is the *successor apostolorum vicarius Christi* (successor of the apostles and vicar of Christ). Preaching as the *praedicatio verbi divini* takes place with the same necessity as that with which the church itself exists, for "God's Word cannot be without God's people and God's people cannot be without God's Word" (Luther). In succession to the apostles, as ministers of the second rank, preachers do in their spheres, i.e., in specific congregations, what the apostles did for the whole church.

As compared to the divine institution of the preacher as *vicarius Christi,* the question of the bearer of the office is a secondary one which can be raised and answered only in relation to the question that is put to the church in every age, namely, whether it is the church of Jesus Christ, so that in it the relation between speaking and hearing is the relation between the speaking of God himself through the lips of the minister and the hearing of his Word in the Holy Spirit. (*Hoc Evangelium ubicumque sincere praedicatur, ibi est regnum Christi. Ubicumque verbum est, ibi est Spiritus Sanctus sive in auditore sive in doctore,* "Wherever this gospel is sincerely preached, there is the reign of Christ. Wherever the Word is, there is the Holy Spirit, whether in hearing or teaching," Luther, *Werke,* Weimar edition, vol. 25, p. 97.) All the concrete marks that we might suggest to prove the authenticity of ministry must be viewed as relative, since they can never be more than human criteria.

Four of the criteria on which, humanly speaking, authenticity is usually made dependent now demand consideration.

1. Ministers should feel inwardly called to their office. They should be aware of the need for this call and give themselves to it wholeheartedly. Nevertheless,

this human "I can do no other" is beset by all kinds of doubts whether basically the supposed inner necessity might not be my own desire. Even the inner call that we think we know carries weight only when it rests on the call of God that we can neither know nor feel.

2. The rules for bishops and deacons in the pastoral epistles (1 Tim. 3:1–7; 3:8–13; 2 Tim. 4:1–5; Titus 1:5–9) contain requirements for the conduct of ministers in the form of lists of Hellenistic virtues. Ministers should be blameless in the sense of not doing what is contrary to prevailing morality. They should not attract unnecessary attention to themselves, and thus detract it from the goodness of the gospel, by overenthusiastic and abnormal participation in the all too human things of this world. These ethical injunctions in the Pastorals ought to make it clear that those who hold these offices must be people who live their lives in the presence of God. But to the extent that the law of God claims them in these commands, they have to confess that they are disobedient at every point. Only those who are justified in Christ are obedient in faith, and only as such do they live their lives in God's presence. But whether they are justified or not cannot be unequivocally determined.

3. The Pastorals also require that the minister should be a *didaktikos* (1 Tim. 3:2; 2 Tim. 2:24). The church has usually taken this to mean that ministers should have academic training in theology. They must not simply rely on the Holy Spirit but strive in all modesty and with all seriousness to interpret the Word correctly even though recognizing that *recte docere* (correct teaching) can become a reality only by the Holy Spirit. It is for this reason that the church cannot responsibly grant anyone the right to proclaim the Word without a theological education. Since, however, the true *didaskalos* (teacher) has to be taught by the Holy Spirit, theological education is only a *conditio sine qua non*.

4. Unlike the apostles the *episkopos* (bishop) is set in a certain place according to the wish of the congregation. Ministry is entrusted to the *ecclesia;* hence there is ministry only *from* the congregation and *to* the congregation. But being called by the congregation does not mean being called by God.

All these four criteria stand related to God's own call, which is beyond our reach. God founds the church. God institutes the ministry and ministers wherever and whenever it pleases him. Ministers, however, must always meet the four criteria behind which, as the ultimate question, there stands the question of their calling by God, which gives force to the criteria but also relativizes them. We can find no answer to this ultimate question. We can only hear it again and again and respond to it in our existence as ministers, so that by our acts it will be evident that there are such things as revelation and the church to which God has given the commission to proclaim it. When this happens, those who are ministers have not to push their own interests, inclinations, convictions, and desires in what they do, nor serve the ideas and movements of their age, though they may also do this. Instead, they must see to it that by their actions it is clear that God has spoken and that God will speak. Where priority is thus given to the divine will and work over a human will and work, they will stand obediently in God's service and authentic Christian preaching will take place.

The conformity of preaching to ministry means that the confidence of the listeners will be gained as they hear from persons of various talents something of that in the service of which the preachers stand. The dubious nature of the action, its sheer impossibility, will always remain, but it has now pleased God to be present himself in and in spite of this human action. As regards preachers themselves, the conformity of preaching to ministry means that they realize how im-

possible their action is, but that they may still look
beyond its uncertainty and focus on the fact of revelation. This will give them confidence that the revealed
will of God which is at work in their action will cover
their weakness and corruptness, and that they are
promised a righteousness which they themselves can
never give to what they do. Knowing the forgiveness
of sins, they may do their work in simple obedience, no
longer, then, as a venture, but in the belief that God has
commanded it.

It must be emphasized that the conformity of
preaching to ministry cannot be clearly described in
psychological terms, whether as regards listener or
preacher. Simplicity and relevance may be the marks of
this kind of preaching but they do not have to be.
Again, the question of success in the sense of a movement and awakening in the congregation cannot be the
criterion of true ministry. Right hearing of God's Word
is the only valid effect of a sermon, but where and
when this happens we cannot know, for what we have
here is the working of the Word of God that we can
only believe.

As the church that is founded on the apostolic word,
the church is never a given factor. It has to be repeatedly founded anew by an apostolic word. It can exist
only in the event of the speaking and hearing of this
apostolic word as God's Word. Thus the church is an
institution only as an invitation, as a waiting for the
church. In the church we are always on the way to the
event of the church. Thus the ministry as the stepping
forth of individuals is an act which must repeatedly
become a reality by the calling of God. Ordination is a
canonical act, but its significance is as a pointer to God's
calling to the extent that in ordination the ordained
come to hear the Word of God, which, however, they
must constantly hear afresh.

The narrower vocation of theologians is not a theological question but a question of ecclesiastical custom. A full divine calling may, of course, stand behind this narrower calling.

In church order and administration only the four criteria that we have adduced apply. Rightly, the church does not permit anyone arrogantly to take up office outside these criteria. Nevertheless, in addition to the *vocatio ordinaria* there is always a *vocatio extraordinaria* (extraordinary vocation). God is not tied to church ordination. He can also call people to proclaim his Word outside the limits of legal ordination. At the same time, the proclamation of those who minister on the basis of an extraordinary calling must be investigated and evaluated by the church to see if it conforms to scripture.

V. Heralding

In considering the essential constitutive elements of preaching, the point in our definition that preaching is an attempt that the church is commanded to make leads us by way of the idea of an attempt to the theme of its provisional character. In this context, however, the usual meaning of the word "provisional" does not exhaust its content. To be sure, the term still has the connotation of that which is not yet definitive. But we must also see that it has a positive sense which must come to decisive expression. In *this* sense "provisional" means "sent in advance," sent on ahead of something that will come later. It is the task of preaching to point to this coming, as the *kēryx,* the herald, intimates the coming of the king whom he precedes.

We arrive here at the real point of transition from the problem of the justification of preaching to the question of its sanctification. Preaching undoubtedly takes

place within a *human* action, but this is an action which
God has commanded and blessed, i.e., to which he has
given a promise. Thus a turn is made here to the morals
or law of preaching. This is why there is an express
relation between the dogmatic concepts of justification
and sanctification. The understanding of preaching as
a human action means for us, of course, an understanding that human beings are neither capable nor worthy
of God. Nevertheless, this action has its own basis and
meaning. Not in itself, of course: Preaching on its own
makes no sense at all. The fact that it has meaning does
not lie in the preaching itself but in the objective substance which is described under points I–IV: revelation,
church, commission, and ministry. This means that
preachers have to rely on the justification of what they
do in Christ, the subject of revelation, the Lord of the
church, the source of the command and calling. They
are thus referred to the necessity of their faith in justification: a faith which grasps it, which stands in strict
relation to the act of the God who justifies that which
does not have justification; faith, then, in the sense:
"Fear not, only believe." Since, however, Christ's justification applies to us in our total existence, it means (in
the sense of *existere*) our justification in the situation of
our stepping out to act, though not as a transformation,
as an endowment, as the infusion of a new nature to
enrich us from some higher source. From first to last
justification is the light of God's countenance on people
who are not transformed, who remain the same as they
were before. Whatever might have to be said about the
new life must all be said with reference to this light.
The final redemption alone will bring the elimination
of the contradiction between the old and the new, the
fulfillment of what we have and are here and now in
promise. Even preaching that is done in faith in God's
turning to us still has of itself the character of a human
action that finally falls under the judgment of him

before whom no one is righteous. Preaching is an attempt that is made with human means. In all circumstances, then, it is made with inadequate means. There
is nothing here upon which to rely. But through God,
who raises up the dead, who calls into being that which
is not, this attempt, this action, is undertaken as a (generally) *good work* insofar as it takes place under God's
command and promise and blessing. Only, then, as it
is justified preaching, done in the light of revelation,
church, commission, and ministry, is preaching a good
work. The last word (which *we* cannot speak) is Jesus
Christ.

We can deal with the question of the law of preaching only when we read off its law from its gospel. We
can ask the question "How can *my* act be good and
holy?" only on the ground of faith, and we can regard
it as legitimate only insofar as it is seen as the reverse
side of what God does for us. A pardoned sinner is
called upon to proclaim the Word of God: What follows when we understand the situation of the sermon
in this way? What is the obedience, the *hypakoē tēs pisteōs*
(obedience of faith), which is the concrete human side
of preaching? What is required is not a specific virtue
but obedience to the undeserved goodness that God has
extended to us. But to look at preaching from this
standpoint, we must focus on the other side of the
definition. Preaching as a human act is claimed by its
basis and meaning. Sanctification means our being
claimed. The new thing that makes the undoubtedly
human but justified act of preaching part of the new
life is this fact that we are claimed. Being claimed by
revelation, church, commission, and ministry, however, does not mean having heard anything at all or
being stirred and moved in any way at all. It means
being addressed by this basis and meaning, by God.
Anyone who thinks we must insert an "only" here does
not know what kind of claiming is at issue or whose

captives we now are. A human being becomes a hearer
of the Word of God: This is our sanctification. The
human being, the preacher, the listener—they are not
left to themselves. They still are what they were before.
But they are not left in peace. As what they are, they
are placed in a *totally* new situation. Anything that we
might say here about the power of God's Word to
create anew is much too weak in view of the rest and
unrest that are present when in faith a human being
may grasp the calling of Jesus Christ. This is God's
turning to us. How, then, should not all things be new?

The focus, however, is on *our* action. What is meant
in practice by this new thing, the new life? *Action* is
at all events demanded: not action on our own but
conscripted action, the action of the slaves that have
a master. This will be an attempt, but that does not
mean that it will be a mere venture, a repeated leap-
ing into the abyss. It is the action of a listener. It is
obedience. What kind of action must it be? It is my
own work, but what must be my attitude if it is to
be an attempt? As preaching is provisional in this way,
its provisional character as such becomes the problem,
the place of conflict and work. In the four points that
follow we shall have to engage in this work and give
an answer to this question—the question of the morals
of preaching.

This brings us to the central key to an understanding
of preaching, the understanding of it as provisional, as
heralding. If we had begun our discussion by seeking
to understand its justification and sanctification, this
would have put us on a path on which everything
would have gone more naturally and smoothly. The
fact that this did not happen might serve as a pointer
to the situation of the church as Christ's handmaid on
earth. A final reference here might well be to a passage
in holy scripture which is often pushed aside as late
Jewish and Hellenistic, though it is really one of the

central parts of the Bible and relates specifically to the situation of the preacher. I have in mind Psalm 119. The 176 verses of this psalm turn over one and the same thing again and again: divine address, justification, joy, and an order, a law, a way.

VI. Scripture

Our fifth point was a general one. It is under the question "What shall we do?" that everything must now stand as we discuss the scriptural character of preaching.

In other words, this means that preaching is exposition of scripture. What must take place in the preaching which is human speech? What is it to offer? If it is a fact that the basis and meaning (or justification) of preaching are to be sought in revelation, church, commission, and ministry, then there can be no question at all of preachers declaiming their own systematic theology or expounding what they think they know about their own lives, or human life in general, or society or the state of the world. If they live by justification, by their faith, it is no longer possible for them to offer systematic theology of this kind, or their own knowledge of how things are and how they ought to be, or ideologies by which people think they may live. Humanity does not live by the immanent goodness of things. When we ask what justifies us, we are referred again to our first four points. We stand before holy scripture. This bears witness to revelation, establishes the church, and gives the command, and vocation comes through it. The act of those who live by justification, then, can be no other than that of understanding and expounding the scriptural word, and to that extent repeating it. To be sure, preachers will always feel the burden of their own systematic theology, but it is one thing to admit this constant threat and another to deny it, one thing to hear and another to reject the claim that even with their own ideas they are set there to expound this book—*that* and nothing else.

In order to avoid generalities we shall now try to describe in five points the approach and qualities of the preacher that correspond to the demand, understood in the above sense, that preaching be an exposition of scripture and not systematic theology.

1. There has to be absolute confidence in holy scripture. If preachers are content to make their sermons expositions of scripture, that is enough. So long as they think that practical life requires more, that the Bible does not suffice to meet what life demands, they do not have this confidence, this *pistis,* and they do not really live by faith.

2. To be an expositor of scripture is to be one who has respect in the sense of *respicere*—to regard. The whole sermon must rest on this *respicere.* The right attitude is that of one who is not concerned with self but with something else, who is so caught up in this situation of *respicere* that there is no time for other things. The sermon will be like the involuntary lip movement of one who is reading with great care, attention, and surprise, more following the letters than reading in the usual sense, all eyes, totally claimed, aware that *"I* have not written the text."

3. Preachers must pay attention to the text, noting what is written in it. From first to last scripture says the same thing, but it constantly says the one thing in different ways. The Bible arose as a historical document speaking of a historical event in the midst of the flux of human life. Instead of attention one might say "diligence," i.e., concern for what is written in this text as in no other. This is why academic exegetical work is

demanded, exact philological and historical study. The variety of scripture has another aspect, namely, that each time each passage will speak as needed to each person. For this reason more than philological attention is needed. Also needed is the attention which is an attempt to read the Word of God in the text and self and congregation. A sermon is not a good one if it is clear that the preacher lacks this attentiveness. For this reason ever new respect or *respicere* to this and that text is required. We must be on guard against the simple indolence that can be natural to even the industrious pastor who is always busy. On Sunday it will become apparent in the pulpit, for no industriousness or activity can compensate for indolence at the decisive point. Church boards should show flexibility in giving pastors more time for preaching, for sermon preparation is time-consuming labor. They should also see to it that only sermons that have been diligently prepared be presented from the pulpit.

4. Preaching that is in conformity with scripture will be modest. Scripture itself enjoins us to be modest, and preachers ought to behave modestly and not to push themselves into the limelight with their more or less good qualities. If the attention to which we referred above is present, the preacher will be under the continuous instruction of scripture, will be contradicted by it, will be kept within bounds. An encounter will take place between the prophets and apostles on the one side and the pastor on the other. The latter must step back with any personal views or spirituality. No matter how vital we may be, we all tend to follow well-defined tracks. Even after the most arduous study, we still do not really know what to say. It can only prepare us for the situation in which God's Word should be spoken. And in this situation we are modest folk who have not yet grasped it. Much might be made of strength or of the power of speech or thought. But these things are

not the gospel. The gospel is not in our thoughts or
hearts; it is in scripture. The dearest habits and best
insights that I have—I must give them all up before
listening. I must not use them to protect myself against
the breakthrough of a knowledge that derives from
scripture. Again and again I must let myself be contradicted. I must let myself be loosened up. I must be able
to surrender everything.

It is especially in relation to this requirement of modesty that one must approach Luther's preaching with
caution. Modesty was not always Luther's strong point.
Out of his great knowledge Luther believed that he had
to say again and again the one thing that motivated
him. He ignored whole complexes of biblical concepts,
e.g., that of law and reward, because he knew only
too well what justification by faith is. To let the text
straighten out our thinking and not to act as those
who are right in the first place—that is what modesty
demands.

5. Finally, preachers must be flexible. The Bible is not
God's Word in the sense of a state code that tells us
precisely what the view of the state is. In reality we
ought to say that the Bible *becomes* God's Word. Whenever it *becomes* God's Word, it *is* God's Word. What we
have here is an event. Simply to have read somewhere
that the Bible is God's Word is not the point. Preachers
are summoned to a life history with the Bible in which
something constantly takes place between them and
God's Word. Flexibility means, then, that we have to
plunge into this movement, submit to it, and let it lead
us through the whole of scripture in all its statements
and stages. The fact of the canon tells us simply that the
church has regarded these scriptures as the place where
we can expect to hear the voice of God. The proper
attitude of preachers does not depend on whether they
hold on to the doctrine of inspiration but on whether
or not they expect God to speak to them here. This

is an active expectation. It is an ongoing submission, a seeking that results in new seeking in return. (The only purpose of testing Bible knowledge in examinations is to find out whether or not the candidate has worked with scripture and is at home in it.) To enter into the movement of the Word is the mobility that is demanded.

These five points regarding the conformity of preaching to scripture have not been heard or understood if they are seen as theological insights which can be evaluated as good or not good. Conformity to the Bible is not a quality that one can "choose." It can be understood only as a discipline under which we are simply placed. We cannot exempt ourselves from this discipline without at once abandoning our ministry in so doing.

Having set forth these five points regarding biblical preaching, I must also refer to *three fatal possibilities,* though these are ruled out if the above demands are heeded.

1. Preachers must not be "clerics" who, puffed up with the sense of their mission, office, and theology, and perhaps "full of the Holy Ghost," attempt to represent the interests of the good Lord to the world. The only healing herb that can meet this vice is that of being biblical, i.e., of engaging in real scriptural exposition. With a biblical attitude and the exposition of scripture we cannot turn into clerics no matter how much we might be inclined to do so. Where holy scripture reigns, no clericalism can develop, and no preacher can be secure or self-satisfied.

2. Preachers must not be visionaries, well-meaning idealists, who push big ideas around in their heads but have no grasp of reality. Preaching that is biblical is never visionary, for holy scripture speaks to reality. In it one may at times feel isolated and lonely, but one need have no fear of one's own dreams and visions.

3. Preachers must not be boring. To a large extent the pastor and boredom are synonymous concepts. Listeners often think that they have heard already what is being said in the pulpit. They have long since known it themselves. The fault certainly does not lie with them alone. Against boredom the only defense is again being biblical. If a sermon is biblical, it will not be boring. Holy scripture is in fact so interesting and has so much that is new and exciting to tell us that listeners cannot even think about dropping off to sleep.

As an afterthought I should also say that the Word of God must remain sovereign and free and thus be able to take its own course. When we are ready to serve the Word of God in this way, with this evaluation of ourselves, the Word of God will be proclaimed, for God will speak his own Word in the congregation.

As regards the handling of Old Testament texts, we maintain that for us the Old Testament is valid only in relation to the New. If the church has declared itself to be the lawful successor of the synagogue, this means that the Old Testament is witness to Christ, before Christ but not without Christ. Each sentence in the Old Testament must be seen in this context. Historical exegesis can and must be done, but at the same time we have to ask whether this exegesis does justice to the context in which the Old and New Testaments stand. Even in a sermon on Judges 6:3 it is possible both to insist on the literal sense and also to set one's sights on Christ. As a wholly Jewish book, the Old Testament is a pointer to Christ. As regards the justification of allegory, we have again to refer to the relation between the Old Testament and the New. In the Old Testament the natural sense is the issue. Preaching must bring out what the Old Testament passage actually says, but in a way that affirms the basic premise on which the church adopted the Old Testament. This does not mean that we will give the passage a second sense—just as we are not to oppose historical and Christian exposition to one another. Instead, we will see that this passage in its immanence points beyond itself. It is a signpost that gives us direction. The Old Testament points forward, the New Testament points backward, and both point to Christ.

The question whether or not one may give a contemporary interpretation to the Pharisee of Luke 7:36ff. is to be answered positively. Preaching is exposition, not exegesis. It follows the text but moves on from it to the preacher's own heart and to the congregation. By means of the Pharisee we may see more closely who might well be meant here, so long as we tie all that is said to the thread of the text.

VII. Originality

Our definition mentions relevance to contemporaries and free human words. By free human words I have in mind originality in preaching. At this point again we are directed to the justification and sanctification of preaching. Sanctification can consist only of this—that preachers just as they are, as sinful human creatures, are called upon to expound the text. Conformity to scripture is not a hood behind which we cannot see the preachers. For a sermon to be biblical does not mean that certain thoughts are given to preachers that they otherwise would not have, after the manner of infused grace *(gratia infusa)*. It is as the persons they are that preachers are called to this task, as these specific people with their own characteristics and histories. It is as the persons they are that they have been selected and called. This is what is meant by originality. Pastors are not to adopt a role. They are not to slip into the clothing of biblical characters. That would be the worst kind of comedy. They are not to be Luthers, churchmen, prophets, visionaries, or the like. They are simply to be themselves, and to expound the text as such. Preaching is the responsible word of a person of our own time. Having heard myself, I am called upon to pass on what I have heard. Even as ministers, it matters that these persons be what they are. They must not put on a character or a robe. They do not have to play a role. It is you who have been commissioned, you, just as you are, not as minister, as pastor or theologian, not under any concealment or cover, but you yourself have simply to discharge this commission.

To this basic discussion of the demand for originality the following specific hints may be appended.

1. In proper sermon preparation the word of scripture has spoken to preachers in such a way that they primarily come before their congregations as themselves hearers.

a. They come before them as those who by this Word have been brought to justice, to penitence, who have themselves specifically been smitten.

b. They come before them as those who have heard the Word thankfully as the gospel, who can concretely rejoice.

Only in this movement through judgment and grace can preaching be truly original.

2. Then there must be the courage to say to others what is now there for *me.* Exegesis and meditation must become speech to others: address, my own speech. I myself am now called upon to be a witness who will remain biblical but will not be stuck fast in exegesis. In this regard we are not to think of explication being followed by application. The so-called introduction is *the* "cliff" in preaching. From the very first sentence, preaching must be address to the people with central communication out of the text.

3. The sermon must be independent. Preachers often have a model in mind. Nevertheless, they must put *themselves* in the pulpit, for *they* are the ones who are called. Even the very best things, when taken over from others, are no longer what they were when spoken by those others. We must not slip into comedy in borrowed robes.

4. Honesty of speech is demanded. Speak your own language! Do not put on the royal mantle of the language of Canaan or pass yourselves off as little Luthers. Precisely those who are committed to exegesis and the church cannot posture as apostles or reformers. Phrases from the Bible and the hymnal and sonorous perorations are not appropriate either. If quotations are introduced only to give momentum to what is said, there is every reason for mistrust. Stand behind your own poverty!

5. Simplicity is needed in a sermon. Preaching ought to be plain and simple. We are to preach as the people we are: in a history, on the way that the Bible takes with us. For this reason we should give honest information and reports about our own situation. This will stop us from unpacking items from a system, or tossing out chunks of Christian thought sequences, or traveling in old ruts. Christian truth is constantly won afresh in history. You must preach as the one you now are today.

Warning: Originality is a dangerous word. It does not imply the "free, independent, converted, born-again personality." It applies to those who live by the forgiveness of sins. Again, it does not mean an existential attitude, for in the ghost of existentialism the old satan of personality hides in a new mask. By paying heed to the demand for originality in a sermon, preachers are protected against becoming pastors of the overconfident, superficial, and halfhearted type.

The independence of preaching does not rule out theological apprenticeship. A theological student, how-

ever, is one who has been taught by teachers to walk
on his own and to handle scripture independently.

VIII. Congregation

If preaching is really justified, then in it we have to
do with the *ekklēsia*. As a preacher I am called upon to
see these people in front of me as God's. This is the
basic presupposition of preaching. If it is in fact God's
will that I should preach to them, how can I address
them except as those for whom God has already acted?
Christ died and rose again for these people in front of
me. It is the truth about them that I have to tell them.
Alētheia (truth) ought to happen. The mystery of God
concerning you should be disclosed. There is mercy for
you. This is as valid now as it was on the first day. It
is in *this* way that preaching must be congregational.
This quality comes to expression in the following individual virtues.

1. Preachers must love their congregations. They
must not want to be without them. They have to realize: I am part of them, and I want to share with them
what I have received from God. It will not help to speak
with the tongue of either men or angels if this love is
missing.

2. If preaching is to be congregational, there must
also be openness to the real situation of the congregation and reflection upon it so as to be able to take it up
into the sermon. Living with their congregations,
preachers live out a history with them, and they are
constantly agitated by the question: "How is it with us
now?" This does not mean that they are to let themselves be carried along by the stream of life and merely
to be the mouthpieces of the *congregation.* They are not

to be popular village sages who know life, who drama-tize it, who tell people what is on their hearts. The sermon is not just a transfigured continuation of life, its leading theme. Life must really be taken up into the sermon. The congregation is waiting for the light of God to shine upon its troubled life, not for the preacher to blow horns that are being blown already. Certainly the preacher is with the congregation, and will be sec-ond to none in sincere solidarity with it, yet for all the solidarity only a certain distance will make a sermon truly congregational.

3. Tact is needed. To have tact is to know what one may say to a congregation in detail. We often think that something *must* be said, even from the Bible, but what it really amounts to is overconfidence, and arbitrary jeopardizing of the relation of trust, and unnecessary offense.

4. At this point a feeling for the *kairos* (Tillich) is also relatively important. What does the situation demand in which we are now together? I live out a history with the congregation. The congregation tells me what is on its heart. My sermon should be a response. This feeling ought to protect us against speaking about things that are no longer important.

From all that has been said it is clear that to be congregational is not to be an information service.

The preacher as tyrant, the pastor as people pleaser, the pastor as recluse—all these may result if the de-mand that preaching be congregational is disregarded.

Note: Biblical criticism in the pulpit also falls under the need for tact. It should be introduced only in the context of ministry and done with respect, not under the pressure of a false ideal of truthfulness.

IX. Spirituality

("Preaching is God's own Word.")
We need the personal God himself. Sanctified preaching should serve God's own Word. Even though we were to do all that has been demanded thus far, we would still be unprofitable servants. Whether or not a sermon is service to the Word depends on whether God himself wills to make use of it.

1. With reference to this event the preacher's attitude must be one of *tapeinophrosynē* (humility).

2. A necessary soberness results from recognition of our humanity vis-à-vis this event.

3. We cannot preach without praying. Since in the last analysis the sermon can have to do with God alone, its words must be spoken in the course of calling upon him, and the congregation, too, must be summoned to pray. But here we have reached the limit of what human beings can say—here at the point where the Spirit himself must represent us with sighing that cannot be uttered.

X. Summary

1. *Revelation*. Preaching has the task of proclaiming the past and future revelation of God, the epiphany and parousia of Jesus Christ.

The past and future revelation of God, set in relation to Jesus Christ, shows that our present lies between the times. The two times cannot be dissolved in a third. Our present stands between the presence of Jesus Christ in the flesh and his coming again with his kingdom. As an event, it is not to be defined or described.

Precisely as such it is always Father, Son, and Holy Spirit. It is not a continuing city but the place of those that are told about the home from which they come and the place to which they are going. Preaching, then, has the task of bearing witness to revelation on its way from yesterday to tomorrow, and thus of taking the way from what has been heard before to what will constantly be heard again. If preaching sounds this basic note, it conforms to revelation and it is in a right relation to the Word of God that it is to proclaim, taking its starting point in this Word and hastening back to it as to something which is wholly new, which constantly renews itself, which is alive.

2. *Church*. Materially, preaching must orient itself solely to baptism as the sign of grace, to the Lord's Supper as the sign of hope, and to scripture as the record of the truth that is the basis of the church.

The place of preaching then, is just not any place we fancy. It is the place which is defined by baptism, the Lord's Supper, and scripture, and by what God does in this sphere. To this place and this place alone preaching must orient itself. Only then can we speak of its conformity to the church.

3. *Confession*. Preaching must edify the church by ongoing discharge of the commission that the Lord has given it.

Confession is the response (the confirmation of reception, as it were) that we make to what we have heard. When there is this response in the church, when it has heeded its Lord's commission, when it confesses itself ready for ongoing discharge of the commission, then the church is repeatedly built up again as it must be from the ground up. This carries with it a commitment to the church's confession.

4. *Ministry*. Preaching takes place on the special authority and responsibility of divine calling to ministry in the church.

Preaching is always a matter of calling. But this is never a human act. Hence all our criteria can only be a pointer to God's own act of instituting the ministry and instituting in it. As God's own deed, this institution is always his own secret, and it thus raises the great question that faces every preacher. The divine calling must justify us, and we know that as we are called we must some day render an account.

5. *Holiness.* Preaching is to be understood as the action of sinners which has its law and promise in the command and the blessing of God.

At this point, which we dealt with as heralding, the reference is to the relation between God and us that takes place in the act of preaching. A sermon is always the work of sinners who have neither the ability nor the will for it but whom God has commanded to do it. Preaching can never be a fulfillment. It can never be more than a precursor. But in view of the promised divine blessing, even though preachers recognize their impotence and inability, nevertheless, on the basis of the command that they have received, they may comfort themselves with the hope that they are not only under law but also under a promise, under God's blessing, so that for all that their work is so pitiable, it will not really be in vain. Only in this sanctification can and may preaching take place.

6. *Scripture.* Preaching as exposition of scripture is in all circumstances under a constraint as regards both form and content. If *the* truth is really to be spoken in the church (see thesis 2), then all that is said in it must take place in the movement and discussion of the record of this truth. Preaching must not be a welling up out of our own speech. In both form and content it must be exposition of scripture.

7. *Originality.* Preaching can take place only in personal repentance and thankfulness, and it is thus a free word of the preacher.

Repetition of the commission that is given to the whole church is a very personal task for preachers to which they must subject themselves. If specific individuals undertake the exposition of scripture, they must themselves have been listening previously to scripture, and they must listen to it over and over again, and do so in a very personal repentance and thankfulness before God. Only in this way can they break through to a free word about scripture. Only in this way can they perform the gigantic task of expounding scripture. In other words, holy scripture first has to break through to them. Only then are they in a position to echo it with their own words and their own thinking.

8. *Congregation*. Preaching aims at the people of a specific time to tell them that their lives have their basis and hope in Jesus Christ.

Since we discussed the concrete situation of the preacher in thesis 7, we will look now only at that of the listeners. The sermon does not take place in a vacuum. It has a human counterpart at which its proclamation is directed, i.e., specific people in a very specific type of present, in a specific place at a specific time. Having a specific hearer to address, a sermon must be very personal. The whole life of the one it addresses has its basis and hope in Jesus Christ. Precisely this person has to grasp this. The proclamation is for this hearer. Naturally, however, we cannot focus on the listeners alone and neglect the place marked out in thesis 2.

9. *Spirituality*. Preaching has to take place in humility and soberness and as the prayer of those that realize that God himself must confess their human word if it is to be God's Word.

Here is the point in the situation of preaching, which we have sought to describe with relative compactness, where it opens up to heaven, and, standing before the mystery of the gracious God, we confess that it is not in our power that our human word should be God's

Word. Preaching, then, must become prayer. It must turn into the seeking and invoking of God, so that ultimately everything depends upon whether God hears and answers our prayer. This opening up to heaven must not be blocked by the triumphant coping of a majestic Gothic arch that shelters us from the gaze of heaven, for we are truly sheltered only when we are exposed before God. There is no place, then, for a victorious confidence in the success of our own action, but only for a willingness to open ourselves to heaven and to remain open to God, so that God himself can now come to us and give us all things richly. Our attitude, then, must be controlled from above: nothing from me, all things from God, no independent achievement, only dependence on God's grace and will.

3
Actual Preparation
of the Sermon

I. Preliminary Remarks

1. THE SITUATION OF (YOUNG) PREACHERS

Let us imagine the situation faced by preachers when they have the task of composing a sermon. Better yet, let us think about the moment when, after finishing their courses and passing their final examinations, theological students reach their goal and as newly ordained ministers have to face their congregations for the first time the following Sunday and preach a sermon. What will it be like? Perhaps a real feeling of joy will run through their souls because the moment has come when they can generously dispense to the assembled congregations the great theological riches that they have amassed over long years of study. They feel that they have something to say. Many good thoughts, very good thoughts, that have been in their minds during the last few days lie ready in the mental drawer waiting to be taken out. All that they have to do is to find the best form in which to communicate them to the people. This is perhaps the mood and the situation of young beginners who find that they have plenty of sermon material during the first years of ministry. But a time will come when they have exhausted this abundance. A time of drought and emptiness will set in which only too easily can discourage and frustrate them. They disconsolately scrape together the few things they still have left to say and realize that sooner or later these fruitful oases will disappear and give way to unrelenting desert.

As regards this second situation, which seems at first glance to be a disaster, it is to be noted that in contrast to the first, which outwardly seems to be more favorable, it is in fact far more fruitful and full of promise. This might at first sound paradoxical, but it is true because preaching is not just speaking and proclamation out of human resources. A dangerous disturbance may result from this erroneous assumption. What counts is not the full supply that I have, the wealth of thought, the more or less brilliant insights. The poor preachers who seem to be facing a blank on Saturday when trying to memorize what seems to be thin and tedious are the very ones who may take comfort. Such preachers need not be alarmed, discouraged, or despairing, for one thing that is told them by way of consolation is that everything is already there that has to be said. This is what we have to realize. In all circumstances all the concerns that burn in on our souls, no matter how pressing, must be repressed.

One thing alone we must do, namely, open our eyes and see the treasure that is spread out before us, and then gather it and draw from the unsearchable riches and pass them on to the congregation. The encouraging "Do not worry" must strike the heart of the discouraged preacher, for the heavenly Father has made provision, and we have simply to be prepared to listen to his Word. Our own inspiration by which we swear in the beginning will leave us in the lurch sooner or later. Then the exposition of scripture must replace it. This alone will endure.

The first step in preparing a sermon is thus to realize

that we must seek the material for it exclusively in the Old Testament and the New. This alone is the material that we must proclaim to the congregation, for as the community of Jesus Christ it is waiting for the food of holy scripture, and nothing else.

2. Text Selection

The term "text selection" has two meanings. It tells us both what *must* be done and what may *not* be done. Every time we choose text we find ourselves deciding between obedience and disobedience, for we fancy that we have some freedom and control as we stand before scripture. Obedience guides our selecting when it is an answer to the claim of God. As it is certainly we ourselves who must choose a text for the sermon out of infinite possibilities available, it is we who must certainly display unconditional obedience in this selection that is a matter of our own judgment. We must not make ourselves masters of the task that is enjoined upon us. We must not act authoritatively or arbitrarily in the selection, for in the last resort it is not we who must hunt around for a text in order to illustrate our own thoughts with its help. For this reason we also misconstrue the task of preaching if we feel compelled to use a text of scripture as the basis for our sermon, the stereotyped introductory formula. This practice downgrades the scriptural saying to the status of a mere motto and misuses it as no more than a springboard for our own world of thought. We should be on guard against picking a text that we can simply exploit. The text itself must always be master, not we.

To avoid mistakes, so far as this is possible:

a. We should not choose texts that are too short, since the danger of arrogance is greater with these than with longer passages. For example, we should not detach the first beatitude from the rest of the Sermon on the Mount. When 1 John 4:16 is the text, it is tempting to take this verse in isolation and to exploit its eloquence instead of letting ourselves be guided by it.

b. We should also be on guard against frequently quoted passages which are supposedly easy to understand. On Reformation Day there is no need arbitrarily to twist the meaning of Galatians 5:1, and on a day of national mourning 1 John 3:16 must not be forced into another context than the biblical one. The illuminating power of a text will always be greater in the divinely given scriptural context than in our own speeches, which may be ever so fine and captivating, but which do violence to the Word.

c. We should not look for allegories, giving the Word more or less beautiful spiritual meanings. We should not practice our own arts with the Word, because the Word that ought to be spoken will not be heard.

d. The sermon should not be for a specific purpose. Thus we should not try to promote church music or start a movement of song by using Psalm 96:1. And at Thanksgiving we should not use the passage in John 4 to discourse brilliantly on the possibilities of harvest. A prerequisite for the apt choice of a text is thus an awareness that we are rendering here a service that we are commanded to perform. Only then may certain other leitmotifs have their place.

Now, in order to avoid mistakes:

a. We may voluntarily follow the prescribed readings, even though much might be said against the ancient church lectionary. When following the readings we are at once compelled to say only what the prescribed text wants, and our own thoughts are held in check. Calvin calls the church the mother of believers, and as a child lets its parents guide it, so a pastor may submit to what the church decides. It is not absolutely necessary, however, to stay on the path suggested by the church.

b. There is also much to be said for doing sermon series, e.g., preaching consecutively on Ephesians, 1 John, etc. In this way we are set under the guidance of the Word. With this model, too, we are less in danger of being "preached out" and having nothing more to say.

c. From constant dealing with the Bible, passages will arise which directly address the preacher. Preachers who live in and with the Bible will know best from this life of theirs what the text imposes and demands. We have to realize, however, that in making these very personal decisions we can go wrong much more easily than in the case of the more external rules of (a) and (b), which, being external, are for that reason all the more dependable.

Pastors ought to seek guidance from scripture more often than for the purpose of preparing their sermons. A profound knowledge of scripture would also reduce the danger of selecting texts that are too short. We cannot view an address on a theme as having the same rank as a sermon on a text (a homily). In the church we do not have the authority to deal with Christian principles or other themes. We have to listen to what is said to the church to found and edify it. No path in the church leads past God's Word. Especially when it wants to win outsiders, by evangelism or missionary work, the church must not deviate from the task that is laid upon it. For this reason it is not good church practice to single out special church events or commemorations. Whether things that the church authorities want particularly mentioned should be noted in a sermon, elaborated, or perhaps totally ignored is not a matter for the preacher but for the claim of the Word of God that is to be expounded. Scripture should purge all our own opinions, desires, and thoughts. In strict discipline we must stay with the Word and be ready to hear only what the Word says, not what the great public, the smaller congregation, or our own heart might like to hear. On special occasions, e.g., the outbreak of war, the text must always stand *above* the theme of the day. Thoughts about the war must not be intruded into the text. More than ever in precisely these situations we must maintain obedience to the text. The church can execute its true task only if it is not caught up in the general excitement but tries to achieve mastery over it by proclaiming what is above all things human. For the same reason we must avoid the use of cliches in the so–called occasional offices. In such cases only the possibility mentioned in (c) is legitimate. The direct inner relation to the content of the Bible and personal involvement in it will offer guidance and at the decisive moment make it clear what is the right text for each specific occasion.

II. The Receptive (Passive) Function

What we have said thus far deals only with what is preliminary to the real work of preparing a sermon. We must now come to grips with the main part of our task: the sermon itself.

Instead of "receptive" (as distinct from "spontaneous") we might say at this point "passive" or "objective" (as distinct from "active" or "subjective"). But we must adopt all such terms with caution. At issue here is the process, in no sense unproblematic, of simply listening to the text, followed by reflection on what to say about what is gleaned from it.

First of all, and very decisively, we must *read the text.* We must get to know word-for-word what is in it, for this must be the content of the sermon. If all that has been said thus far is understood, this will be self-evident.

In this regard, however, we must observe two rules.

1. First, to gain acquaintance with the selected passage of scripture we must always use the original. We must use this first, not avoiding the effort of translation from the Hebrew and the Greek. Superficially this might seem to be unnecessary and time-consuming, but all translations, no matter how excellent or authentic, suffer the weakness of being secondary. A translation is not the original, the source. It has the features of an exposition or commentary. To understand fully the written Word we must take the path from the true source to the broad stream of interpretation. Any detour will mean that we miss part of the full journey.

Now obviously we cannot say that Hebrew and Greek are specially adapted to serve as languages for the Bible as God's Word. The Holy Spirit has no language of his own. It should no longer strike us as a problem that holy scripture is given to us in particular forms of the human power of expression. If asked why these languages in particular were predestined, we can only reply: "That is the way it is." We just have to accept it. A sermon will give evidence whether or not it was prepared from the original source. If it was, the text will be seen in the light of that other language because relations will emerge that would not otherwise be apparent. Only then may we reach for textual aids, and first of all for translations.* As regards the New Testament, we might mention especially Adolf Schlatter's version, which will always be read with profit even when we do not agree with him. We might also mention the translations of Weizsäcker and C. Stage. Luther's version will always occupy a place of special honor. It is in fact the one in which church members with no theological training will have the Bible and it

---

*Barth naturally gives translations in German, with special emphasis on the Luther Bible.—Trans.

has been read for centuries in the churches. For this reason we must lend our ears especially to this voice. On the whole it is to be recommended that we not read our own renderings in the pulpit and that we deviate from Luther only when he misses the sense. In cases in which he does not quite catch the nuance, there will be adequate opportunity to go into this in the sermon. Otherwise it must be accepted that Luther was a translator of great knowledge and understanding.

2. When we have read the text our next step is to inquire into its *content.* We must ascertain first the context in which the selected passage stands, for each text has an organic connection with the whole biblical corpus; it does not exist in isolation. We need to see clearly and surely what is the material both before and after to which this passage is indissolubly related. The whence and whither of a text are not only a concern in academic exegesis; they are also not to be overlooked in any homiletical work. Many sermons would have a different look if they had been composed with a knowledge of what comes before the text and what comes after it.

Then we must analyze the text. Attention should focus on certain features that are in some sense to be viewed as stating in part the purpose of what is said in the text, namely, on the proportions of the statements, the order of the concepts, and the drift of the text. Only then should commentaries be used.

The difference between a commentary and a translation is that the commentary discusses the individual components of the text. In choosing a commentary we find that there are two basic types. Modern commentaries from the eighteenth century onward stand under the sign of historical-critical research. Faced with them, many moderns feel they have to read the Bible after the historical-critical manner. This is a possible way of reading the Bible that older commentators also knew.

It means focusing on the historical or earthly form of the Bible. An attempt is made to understand it as it is concretely. This endeavor is so self-evident and justifiable that no more need be said. It has been known all along that the Bible did not fall from heaven. It has a wholly natural historical genesis. Paul, for example, was a child of his time and could speak only as such. The only point is that the older expositors took much less seriously the restrictions that such an understanding of the Bible might impose. Today, however, this understanding of scripture has been subject to hypertrophy by trying to communicate the truth of scripture as though the historical meaning of the text were its total sense.

We have here a dogma—not a church dogma but a pagan dogma—which recognizes only humanity and its world and functions, among which is religion. This dogma, however, cannot be the presupposition of preaching. If it is true, then commitment specifically to the *Bible* no longer makes sense. Many other texts are of equal concern to us. What holy scripture is all about deep down and in the last analysis we can recognize only when we see that it is not primarily a historical document but first and supremely it is testimony to the one and only revelation of God, the Word of God himself.

All the same, we must read commentaries that are the product of historical-critical research, e.g., such works as Lietzmann's *Handbuch,* the *Göttinger Bibelwerk,* and the commentaries of Jülicher, Zahn, and Holtzmann. If today more attention is paid to the human form of the Bible, we cannot ignore this. Commentaries of this type are no danger to us so long as we are alert. We know very well that the Bible *is* a historical document, but that it only is this *also.* In the whole sphere of revelation the truth holds good that the Word became flesh. It really became a historical document.

The problem is this: How far is this wholly concrete human word the Word of God, witness to the Word of God? How far is something said in this text that points beyond the human to the God who wills to act with us? How far is there a movement in which the writer looks beyond his deepest human emotions to Immanuel? No critical question can prevent us from seeing this and taking it just as seriously. The Word became *flesh,* but the *Word* became flesh. This is the Christian dogma of the Bible. The human beings who speak in it are subject to the truth that has come upon them. On the basis of revelation they speak about revelation. The modern commentaries cannot tell us this. On this question the older exegetes are more dependable. It is inadvisable to use only the modern ones, and in this regard it should be noted that the modern conservative ones are not equal to the older commentaries, since they are often so similar to liberal ones, even to the point of confusion with them.

Older commentaries that particularly call for notice are Bengel's *Gnomon Novi Testamenti,* the expositions of Calvin and Luther, and also Augustine, though some caution is needed in using him. We might also consider reading sermons on the chosen text. In this regard modern sermons must be read with special care, since they all stand under the fatal sign of the "theme" sermon. Nevertheless, there are sermons in print which are really good, so that we can turn to them without a qualm and use them as a kind of commentary. The fact is that there has always been a wrestling for true understanding of the Bible among pastors. Why, then, should we not go to school with them and learn from them? The sermons of Hermann Friedrich Kohlbrügge, Gottfried Menken, and Calvin all have the unequivocal character of scriptural exposition.

Finally, then, we would make it a rule to use old as well as new commentaries, to place them side by side, to test everything, and to keep what is good. Above all things human, the point is always to be an echo for the call of God that comes to us in his Word. Any impulses that come to us from other sources can never be anything more than that.

Afterthoughts. Should the time for sermon preparation be very limited for reasons beyond our control, at the very least we must read the text both in the original and in Luther's translation. We should take this course only in emergencies. We who in contrast to the Roman Catholic Church have the true sanctuary, the Word, must see and execute in sermon preparation and the sermon itself the real task of pastoral work which is also its point.

How can I preach from an inauthentic text which I know from historical criticism to be legend and myth, thus assuming it to be secondary in the New Testament? The answer is that no one can preach, of course, on a legend. But since I come upon the text in the church, and am called upon to hear *God's* Word in it, no historian's judgment can make this text unserviceable as the Word of God.

III. The Spontaneous (Active) Function

We now come to the second function, which we have called spontaneous, active, or subjective. Much more must be said about this function because our truly effective and responsible work is included here. We will divide our discussion into two parts under two main heads: (1) The way of witness, and (2) The actual situation of the text.

1. The Way of Witness

When the so-called passive way that we have just depicted has been pursued, when the text has been read and a better understanding of it sought by reading older and modern commentaries, the preacher faces a decision resulting from the fact that the Bible is both a historical book and a church book. As a historical book it is the monument to a piece of the history of human piety. This is the point that modern commentaries have made so sharply and faithfully. But for preachers and readers of the Bible in the Christian church it is not enough to view the Bible as a monument of this kind, i.e., as the monument that reminds us of something past, of something that once was. This does not exhaust the Bible's significance. We also see something else, something much more important, in it. It is a document, a writing, a record, the validity of which has been upheld unchanged to the present day, and which also confronts the present age with a decision, offering it a command, a commission, a directive—a record of a decision which was made in the past but which is still in force today. The text as part of the Bible is thus primarily important to us as a document, a record. But let us add at once: Not just as a record or document that had authoritative significance for some group at a particular time, but one that very specially and exclusively speaks to none other than precisely us at this particular moment, and does so as the one and only witness to the revelation of God, a Word which God has spoken to this age.

a. *Theme, or Scopus?*

Since the Bible has this character it is absolutely impossible for us to ask concerning the theme, or *scopus,* of the individual passage. In the Christian church the

Bible is the witness to God's revelation. As the only, yet also the all-sufficient, witness to God's revelation, we call holy scripture itself the Word of God which has been spoken and which will be passed on by heralds in preaching. When the Bible is understood thus as witness to God's Word, as witness to a decision, an act of God, then it seems to be impossible to begin examining the text that has just been read and academically studied in search of its theme, or *scopus*. The answer to such questions would be that throughout the Bible there is only a single theme, namely, God's own Word, his revelation, Jesus Christ himself. The blunder of positing any other theme would be nothing other than an arrogant but futile attempt to bring Jesus Christ on the scene, as it were, by our own deliberations.

Jesus Christ is not simply present in the Bible. He is not simply to be found in preaching. What is present in the biblical text and can be passed on is something very different. It is not revelation itself, but witness to God's revelation. This witness is not the theme of the Bible. It is a human statement made by the prophets and apostles, who did not speak of themselves but who were forced, as Paul says, or who had to carry a burden, as the prophets say, a burden about which they spoke as best they could, in responsibility to those to whom they spoke the Word of God. The text on which the preacher is to preach is part of their train of thought under this responsibility.

We call this train of thought the way of witness. The text does not consist of individual sayings. It is in a context. This is why we must be warned over and over again against preaching on short texts, for with such texts we more easily neglect the context. John 1:7f. shows us clearly what a witness is. Note here *martyrein peri autou* (bear witness to it). The witness speaks about that to which it bears witness. It is not itself the object of its witness. John the Baptist was not the light; he bore witness to the light: "Behold the Lamb of God, that bears the sin of the world."

As regards the content of a sermon, we define it thus: The content of a sermon is a repetition of the *martyria* that was written once and for all in the Bible by a person of our own time who offers the repetition, but always with a focus on the apostles and prophets, etc. The sermon should never have as its subject familiar truths such as the grandeur of faith, or Christ and country, etc., or known or relatively little-known truths that are sought and found in the Bible. Instead, it must point to the truth that is absolutely unknown, and do so with the hope and prayer that this truth, the *alētheia Iēsou Christou* (truth of Jesus Christ), will now itself speak and make itself known through the ministry of this simple reference. We must always keep this in view as the point of preaching, namely, that behind the biblical text stands the truth that is absolutely unknown to humans but that wills to disclose itself, making itself the absolutely known truth by the call of the church. To theologians no less than laity this truth is the hidden truth. We theologians have merely to repeat what these people said about that which encountered them. When we do this simply and modestly, we serve God's own Word. May it be that as we hear their word we may hear the Word of him who alone can make it heard. To preach is to tread again with the congregation the way of witness taken by the text. Here the very great burden of the mystery of revelation is lifted from us. What the prophets and apostles heard, we must try to repeat.

Three points may be added which are in some sense technical explanations of what has just been said about the way of witness in the text.

b. *Three Technical Explanations*

i. The biblical Word is both document and monument. We must take note of the fact that it is the monument of a piece of the history of piety. If in preaching we attempt to follow the first witnesses obediently, simply to repeat what they once had to say to the world, we must always remember that the object of this repetition should not be the external form of the witness, its historical dress. When the repetition of a document is at issue, we do not always have to repeat the monument. The historical element cannot have an autonomous place in the sermon. Historical information will always be a burden in preaching. We should refer to historical aspects only insofar as they belong intrinsically to the witness and the witness cannot be repeated in any other way. In a sermon we have to tread the way of witness in today's situation. We must learn its direction from the text but follow it in our own situation. This will impose a limit on too strong an accentuation of historical events in preaching.

ii. Something that we can fully understand psychologically is that having found a way of witness and made it our own we want to follow it again and again, restricting ourselves by a definite decision to the same track. A warning is needed then, lest the preacher, neglecting the great wealth of ways of witness in scripture, becomes stuck on the way that is once discovered, thus composing every sermon according to the same pattern. Students should be counseled to look at the Bible as a multifaceted book. No single pattern should be followed in every sermon, e.g., that of the sinfulness of humanity, the appearance of Christ, the need for human improvement. Scripture is like a great forest or ocean in which each tree or drop is something special. This variety completely rules out boredom and helps us avoid well-worn tracks and strike out repeatedly on new paths. If we take heed of this warning, then we will know how to say something fresh each Sunday and point to the great new thing, to the great new beginning that we may make with God on the basis of his great new beginning with us.

iii. In order to avoid the danger of an arbitrary biblicism, we must constantly remind ourselves that preaching takes place in a very specific church at a very specific time. Here, then, we must seriously point out how important it is to work carefully on the dogmatic history and dogmatics of the church within which preachers must engage in proclamation at their own particular location. All preachers need a good dogmatics. In this regard attention should be drawn to the extraordinary importance of dogmatic studies at the university and later in the ministry. For an understanding of the Bible we need particular guidelines which like buoys in the sea mark off the channel, and sometimes detours as well, but always serve to protect us against running aground through ignorance or negligence. To use another comparison, we must not blunder willfully through the great forest of the Bible, shooting at random, but follow a course that is set for us by dogmatics ancient and modern. In so doing, we are not to introduce dogmas into a sermon word for word, and in the process show off our learning. We should let them be signposts from which to take direction. Reflection upon dogma will guard us against our own imaginings. Dogma is a good pair of glasses with the help of which we can look at the text cheerfully and confidently. Doing this will save us from caprice, but we must do it with discipline and a sense of responsibility that is firmly based on the church.

To show what all this means in practice, we will now work out some sermon sketches.

c. *Three Sermon Sketches*

Psalm 121

This psalm falls into four parts. (1) Verses 1f. The psalm is a pilgrim song. It has as its content the problem of help. The psalmist is weak and helpless but knows both that help is available and also the place from which it comes. With the confidence of faith he lifts up his eyes to this place, to Jerusalem, where the Lord God, the Almighty, the Creator of heaven and earth, has his dwelling. From there help comes to him. For us this means that we, too, have a place from which help may be expected. (2) Verses 3f. This certainty is based on the conviction that the God who gives help is supremely active. We know that he never sleeps and therefore that he is never beyond the reach of those in need of help. He does not lead a life that is no use to us because he is absent or far away. On the contrary, the Lord is always present, as close as close can be, and we have him always by us. (3) Verses 5f. Precisely, then, when the danger is greatest and we are under the threat of perishing, the Lord protects us. There is a danger based on our cosmic condition as human beings from which we cannot escape on our own. But here specifically we are told of God's protection very positively and in the indicative mood. (4) Verses 7f. The indicative now changes into the optative, into prayer. The Old Testament congregation would pray for each individual member, and in this intercession for one another find strength and comfort. We today also know that prayer is being made for us, but there is a much more efficacious prayer now than then: Jesus Christ himself intercedes for us in the presence of Almighty God. His prayer is our hope. This is roughly how the sermon might go. It will be seen that there is no specific theme.

John 13:33–35

These three verses might be an appropriate text for a
Passiontide sermon. Here as always we must pay close
attention to what comes before and after the passage.
The *exēlthen* (Judas!) in verse 30 ("he went out") signifies the start of the final climax in the passion of the Son
of Man. The text opens with a salvation-history *present:*
"Now is the Son of Man glorified!" But this glorifica-
tion takes place in the night, not just outwardly, but in
the night of Christ's passion. The time has come when
the incarnation, and consequently God's self-hum-
bling, comes to fulfillment. This moment already
denotes the step to Christ's exaltation. *Now* is the Son
of Man glorified!—and God will then glorify him in
himself; verses 31 and 32 go closely together. On the
other hand, in verse 33 there is a distinctive delay. Jesus
tells his disciples: "Where I go, you cannot come." The
whole community of believers is present in these few
apostles. Jesus shares his thoughts with them. They
must all know and understand that they cannot walk
the path that Jesus is taking. Neither the world nor the
church will ever be able to imitate what he, Christ
alone, was singled out to do. Only he and no one else
will tread the way to the Father—and do so *for* the whole
world. If there can be no imitation of Christ in this
respect, something else is all the more urgently commanded: Obedience. "A new commandment I give you,
that you love one another." Good Friday and Easter,
those stations on the way of Christ, are stations of love.
An event took place here that put to death all enmity
and lovelessness. The ground was thus cut away from
under all our hatred. Acknowledgment of this new situation is obviously the same for us as acknowledgment
of the new commandment of love. Where, then, this
commandment is concretely obeyed, it will be seen that
there are people who have been to school with Jesus

Christ and learned there his significance for their lives. We are not told that by the behavior of these pupils the whole world will be won for Christ, but only that people will say to one another: "These are followers of Jesus who look and live like this." When we rightly take thoughts such as these from the passage and put them in our sermon, in face of them we will seek in vain for a single underlying theme. The task is this—to repeat in our own terms for our own people what is there in the text. In any event a superabundant fullness is to be found in these few verses.

Ephesians 2:1–10

The problem of preaching on sin is acute here. It is stated initially (verses 1–3) that all those to whom the apostle is speaking, the cosmic, worldly people entangled in sin, once lived as autonomous beings in this condition. But this state of transgression and sin could not be compared to real life. Instead, in the truest sense they were dead under the wrath of God. In verse 3, which especially emphasizes sin in all its terrible concreteness, a noteworthy transition is made from the "you" (plural) to a sudden "we." In this way Paul deliberately includes himself in sin. But the totality of sin—we must not overlook this—is put in the past. This in no way weakens the sense of sin. On the contrary, the terrible nature of sin is particularly highlighted by the past tense. Although we all know from experience how completely this past impinges on the present, it is nonetheless true that God has long since thrown this frightful present back into the past. The reason why the Christian church can manage to talk about sin with this apparent confusion of tenses is to be found in the Easter message with which verse 4 begins: "But God who is rich in mercy." Every human "But" is silenced in advance by this divine "But." In the church of Christ then, we do not look on the serpent

whose fierce bites wound us again and again but on the
serpent which is lifted up and a glance at which brings
healing to every wound.

Verses 4–7 present the Victor over all that is called
sin. The joyful message is this: All you who were dead
in bondage to sin are now raised with Christ. This
raising of the dead, however, is only a work of God
himself, accomplished in Christ and his exaltation. The
fight against sin is long since over. The battle has been
won. Victory is sure. This was the way in which Paul
fought evil. Not by morality, not by ethical rules, but
simply by a reference to him who once and for all
robbed sin of its power. This focus on Christ is the
theme of verse 7. In the Christian, Paul sees the object
of the goodness of God which out of his boundless
riches has prepared for us an everlasting inheritance.
Verses 8–10 put us in the time between the resurrection
and the second coming. Whatever we are between the
times is not of ourselves. We have no cause or right to
boast. It is not by our works that we are what we are.
On the contrary, we are saved by grace through faith,
and we have faith, too, only as the gift of God. Nevertheless, we are created for good works in which we are
to walk. It is significant that Paul avoids the imperative
here and presents facts in the indicative. His concern is
to leave us in no doubt that it is all God's work and
none of ours. Those who seek the essential imperative
here will have to find it precisely in the indicative.

These verses are a pregnant part of the apostolic
testimony which has no real theme but which stands
under the great theme of the Bible—and it is to the
proclamation of *this* testimony that the Christian community has a claim.

2. ACTUAL SITUATION OF THE TEXT

a. *Explication and Application*

If we now see clearly that the proclamation of the Word can be no more than a simple repetition of the witness that is given to us in scripture, the task takes on a broader dimension inasmuch as we have to follow this way of witness into the *present.* In what surroundings do we have to make our journey? We must ask ourselves this question because the witness in scripture is not tied to a single period but is given to the church of the present, i.e., to people who are called by the Word of God and will be called over and over again. In other words, the witness of holy scripture speaks to the world which is to become the church. This is the divine side of holy scripture. The address does not imply any special election—the witness is to be given to all. This need, which is restricted to no one period or generation, raises the question of speech, i.e., of the possibility of passing on what we are commanded to say. For preaching is not to be explication alone. It may not be limited to exposition with no regard for the hearers. Something more must be done. Every sermon must also take the form of application. An exposition, no matter how true to the text, will die away ineffectually in a vacuum if there is no possibility of a responsive echo from those who hear it. When we take into account the listeners and their individuality, the question of the "how" of proclamation becomes a very large and important one for us. We must see to it as best we can that our sermon does not turn into a monologue which is beautiful but of no use to the congregation. If it is this, its life is already over. The preacher is not isolated when he proclaims the Word as a herald. It is part of the office to be very sensitive to the congregation and very intimately bound up with it. If follows, then, that there is

a need to make a unity out of the duality of exposition
and application.

The people I wish to address must be in my mind's
eye as I prepare my sermon. Much will depend on
whether I know them well or not. From my knowledge
of them there will emerge insights and associations that
will be with me verse by verse in my preparation. These
insights provide the contemporary material of the sermon. And if the findings of our theological exegesis
give us the unshakable foundation, the contemporary
material provides the uncertain and relative element in
the construction of the sermon. In describing the relation between exposition and application in sermon
preparation, the following principle holds good: In a
sermon, explication must relate to application as subject does to predicate.

b. *The Methodological Way*

Purely methodologically, the way to proceed is as
follows. First, we should simply write down the ideas
that come to mind while we are thinking about the text.
But at once we must sound a warning. To a greater or
lesser extent the contemporary material that we have
collected has a very uncertain and changeable character. We have to take this into account in our sermon
preparation. In contrast, the pure textual offerings, un-
burdened by any human admixture, will prove to be
the only sure and reliable foundation. Now as ever they
are the alpha and omega of the way of witness that we
must walk. Only when we see and accept this can we
profitably exploit the second recognition, namely, that
we must walk this way of witness in and with the
present-day church, and that this is the church which
has been called already but which is repeatedly to be
called afresh. The people we address are people with all
kinds of anxieties and needs. It is in this very concrete

situation of their earthly condition and situation that the call of Jesus Christ comes to them as people of the present age. Neither preacher nor congregation must be viewed as an abstract entity. The church does not find embodiment in the person of the preacher or in the congregation. It is *both* preacher *and* congregation. The two form a unity that is not to be put asunder.

By the present-day people who are at issue in application, we are not to understand either the preacher alone or the congregation abstractly without the preacher but the preacher in the congregation or the congregation in which the preacher stands. The sermon, then, cannot on the one hand be a soliloquy of the preacher on himself and his sins, for this would mean the elimination of the church as the communion of saints. But the danger of aberration is greater on the other side, for it can easily happen that the proclaimer of the Word of God overstresses the distinction between preacher and people in the other direction and thus thinks he must abstractly address the congregation without including himself in it. What we need to realize about the situation of the preacher is that he, too, belongs to the congregation, certainly as the bearer of an office, but of an office that was given him by the congregation, so that he must never feel superior to the congregation, but see that he is set within it as one who must also simply hear the Word of God again and again. Recognition of this situation of the preacher is the basic prerequisite for the proper application of the Word, which at the same time can never cease to be explication.

When we consider that preaching is a matter of following the way of witness demanded by the text, further reflection on the nature of application runs into a difficulty which we can only describe and not solve. The problem is that of the relation between closeness to life and closeness to the text.

When preparing their sermons, preachers have to meditate on the texts both as genuinely people of their day but also in such a way that the text can really become a Word to their contemporaries. As we have seen, the postulated and contemporary material has to be related to the text that is studied. This means that two limits are set as we fashion and evaluate the material that has been amassed: an *optimum* and a *pessimum.* The decision how far the text can allow the inclusion of present-day problems always results in an upper limit to the degree that scripture is accepted as the only norm. If, however, preachers lose themselves in their own thoughts without setting a scriptural limit, we are faced with a very dubious fulfillment of the postulate of application. We have to say on the one hand that when preparing a sermon we cannot think enough about the people for whom it is meant. Each word that is to be proclaimed to the listeners must become a Word that is specifically and decisively addressed to our own present.

But woe to preachers who do not see first how relevant the Word of the Bible is to the people of today! Woe even more to preachers who do see the contingency* and relevance of the biblical Word to the people of today but who are then fearful or unwilling to give offense and thus become deserters of the Word—the Word which seeks to seize and disturb and confront the people of today, and in this way to lead them truly to the rest of God, but which is buried by the cowardice and disobedience of the preachers, and thus prevented from doing its proper work! This is why proper application of the text demands a certain ordinary courage— the courage that simply wants to help the content of the Word to find expression in all circumstances vis-à-

---

*For this use of contingency cf. *Church Dogmatics* I/1, 5.3.1 (1st ed., pp. 164, 169f.; 2nd ed., pp. 145, 149f.).—Trans.

vis life's external relations, a courage, then, which in obedience to the text ventures an assault on the concrete situation of life, and which is spared any responsibility for the consequences of this assault that is launched in obedience to the Word of scripture. For in this case it is the Word of scripture alone that bears the responsibility. For responsible pastors there is no time or situation whatever in which the text might be threatening or dangerous. What the text has to say may be said unconditionally even if it costs the preacher his neck. Openness to the text and the courage to proclaim it—this is what we must emphasize as strongly as possible at this point.

The demand for closeness to life goes hand in hand with the demand for closeness to the text. But precisely when we take it with full seriousness we run up against a difficulty for which there is no particular solution but which is so dangerous that we must describe it by way of warning. The great danger is that, on the basis of the thought associations which in our view have come to us in our exposition of the text as connections to the reality of people today, something will be intruded into the text from outside which is not in the text itself but which we think we must unconditionally bring into the sermon because of a certain intoxication with the beauty of the thought. Thus, while we do not succumb to the mistake of an exegesis that is remote from life, we fall into the bigger and more serious mistake of blowing mental bubbles, i.e., of wresting the text, or, in short, of theme preaching, in which something that is secondary in the text can only too easily become the main thing in the sermon, since we only too willingly confuse the beautiful thoughts of our self-seeking ego with thoughts of the text, which are usually less comfortable and less in keeping with the thinking of the age.

For this reason it is important that we take the con-

temporary material that crowds in upon us and reex-
amine it in the light of the text, putting it through a
second filter as it were, even though we earlier called
this type of caution inappropriate when it was a matter
of openness to the text and the courage to proclaim it.
The caution in exposition which finds expression in the
demand for the unity of exposition and application can
often mean that the finest thoughts that come to us
when reading the text must finally be jettisoned, on
further scrutiny of the text, as textually out of keeping
with the way of witness that the Word of scripture
itself prescribes. In some circumstances even the main
thought may have to be sacrificed if closer examination
proves it to be superfluous and arbitrarily intruded
material.

But it will undoubtedly be a sacrifice that is pleasing
to God if we do not proudly and stubbornly insist on
thoughts that really are not pertinent to the subject.
Preaching which after this type of preparation is not
ashamed to come with broken limbs cannot be called
either cowardly or inappropriate, i.e., not in conformity
with the text. The right kind of courage *(Mut)* before
both text and people, and also the right kind of humility *(Demut)* before the text, i.e., the necessary objectivity
vis-à-vis holy scripture, will then be present, and only
then can the sermon be a means of blessing. It is precisely here, however, that the difficulty lies in the relation between explication and application, namely, in
the tension between closeness to life and closeness to
the text, between courage in relation to the text and
humility or caution in face of it. No principle can re-
solve this tension. No more is possible here than the
movement from courage to humility or vice versa. Both
must always be taken into account, though with a different accent. As regards the general question of the
greater dignity of the one or the other, however, there
must be a slight tilt in favor of humility, as in the

relation between love of God and love of neighbor. For in preaching it is always better to be too close to the text than to be too thematic or too much in keeping with the times. Of two evils, it is better here to choose the lesser. Three little warnings arise in this connection.

c. *Three Warnings*

i. What does it mean to "apply" a text? What does it mean to witness to people today on the basis of a text? At all events it does not mean adducing quotations from the newspaper with more or less relevant contents, or merely alluding to them with the aid of catchwords. A direct approach of this kind does little to give a sermon the congregational character that we demanded at the outset. What is perhaps lauded as effective, e.g., a regional or local sermon, can be very harmful. This kind of model will not give us the decisive thing. It is even conceivable that preachers who compose their sermons along strictly exegetical lines and do not refer to the present day at all, but whose hearts are burdened with the thousand problems of the age, will have a genuine closeness to life. We should not always assume that the congregation, especially in a farming community, is so ignorant of the world and so far removed from life that it has no knowledge of the ills of our day. It has a very good knowledge of life and does not need orientation from the pastor. Let us always pay heed then, to the great danger of direct speech and allusion as such. Association with external thoughts of this kind often results in the listeners wandering off on thoughts of their own. Especially unhelpful is the method of seasoning a sermon with all kinds of illustrations. In no circumstances should we hunt around for these!

ii. All of us, especially those who are preachers, have our favorite theoretical and practical thoughts that we find it hard to discard. Application should not consist of giving free rein to such thoughts. These thoughts are part of the flesh, of the old unbaptized nature. Here and there, perhaps, there might be a situation in which we can express them, but the danger of misuse is gigantic. The hobbyhorse of total abstinence for example, or other social and ethical problems, will always be there to seduce a preacher into having a shot at them. Caution is thus needed in relation to our pet ideas. What is required is a readiness to break through to the text.

iii. Another warning is to be sounded at this point. The application or reference does not always have to be *à jour*. We do not always have to bring in the latest and most sensational events. For instance, if a fire broke out in the community last week, and church members are still suffering under its awful impact, we should be on guard against even hinting at this theme in the sermon. It belongs to everyday life, but now it is Sunday, and people do not want to remain stuck in everyday problems. They want to go beyond them and rise above them.

In my parish work in Switzerland I often fell into this danger of misunderstanding how preaching is to be congregational. In 1912, when the sinking of the Titanic shocked the world, the next Sunday I had to make this disaster the main theme of my sermon, and a monster of a full-scale Titanic sermon resulted.

Again in 1914, when the outbreak of war left the whole world breathless, I felt obliged to let this war rage on in all my sermons until finally a woman came up to me and begged me for once to talk about something else and not constantly about this terrible conflict. She was right! I had disgracefully forgotten the importance of submission to the text. It may come to the point that a member of the congregation has to call the pastor to order and counsel reconsideration. All honor to relevance, but pastors should be good marks-men who aim their guns beyond the hill of relevance.

3. WRITING THE SERMON

The basic prerequisite in execution is to write the sermon. This condition is so important that a thorough argument in its favor seems to be needed. To be sure, a sermon is a speech. It has to be this. But in this speech we should not leave it up to the Holy Spirit (or some other spirit!) to inspire the words, no matter whether we have an aptitude for speaking or not. Instead, a sermon is a speech which we have prepared word for word and written down. This alone accords with its dignity. If it is true in general that we must give an account of every idle word, we must do so especially in our preaching. For preaching is not an art that some can master because they are good speakers and others only by working out the sermon in writing. The sermon is a liturgical event. It is the central act of Protestant wor-ship, closely related to the sacrament. Only a sermon in which each word is fully accounted for is a sacramental act. Those who have to lead the worship of the congre-gation and perform the central act, which corresponds to the sacrifice of the Mass in the Roman Catholic Church, should realize that they can engage in this ministry only after full reflection, to the very best of their knowledge, and with a clear conscience. Each ser-mon should be ready for print, as it were, before it is delivered. A sermon is more than a lecture, a Bible lesson, or a confirmation class, and we must conduct ourselves accordingly. It is part of the sanctification of the preacher to feel bound once and for all to this rule.

This demand is an absolute rule for all. We may rob it of its universal validity by applying it only to young preachers until they have had the necessary practice.

There is a great danger in this type of thinking. Hundreds and thousands of pastors have had practice enough, but even so—or just because of it—their sermons are only religious addresses. By this rule we are not condemning anyone, but we have set ourselves the task of considering what is right for one who is not a prophet but must prepare sermons with prayer and toil.

Let us now focus on the purely linguistic form of the Word that we are to proclaim. We might speak here of the need to nurture speech. Just as cultivation is a needed sphere of life, we can never do enough to cultivate the organ of speech. There is a process of grinding language down which results in our repeating ourselves—using set phrases for certain things. But this leads to people missing what we are saying. An emphatic warning must be given against trying to impress the listener by constant repetition of hackneyed terms. Repetition always robs the content of its force. Shallow reading and newspaper jargon are a danger because they can poison our language from without with their general expressions and modish turns of phrase, which in many cases are totally meaningless. By overhasty and superficial writing we risk ruining the language and letting clichés become a regular disease. The only way to avert this danger is painfully to work on every single word that we ought to use in the sermon. By this work, which cannot be merely a matter of thought, we learn to pay attention to phrases and sentences. There will be many salutary checks. At the same time, writing is creative production, and in view of the high purpose it is good to don here a festive robe. The sermon demands an orderly language which is appropriate from the standpoint of content as well as expression. Form and content, then, are not to be separated in preaching. The right form is part of the right content.

4. Unity of the Sermon

As regards the actual execution, the following points are to be noted.

a. *Totality*

As we have seen, a sermon is both the explication and the application of the text. Basically this applies to the whole sermon, which constitutes in some sense a single body. A division into parts, therefore, is a mistake. It breaks the unity of the sermon. The totality of the sermon is constituted by the totality of the given text. The unity lies in the text itself and should find expression in the sermon, which follows the movement of the text. There is no need, then, to consider the problem of what should come first, second, and third. The preacher has only to repeat what the text says— and this is one thing. The one thing is the Word of God. It is Jesus Christ. We ourselves cannot produce this or contribute to it. We can only bear witness to it, to the one thing which is the corpus of the text.

b. *Introduction?*

Basically the sermon should not have an introduction. Only one kind of legitimate introduction is conceivable. When a scripture reading precedes the sermon, a link can be made with this, so that in some sense the sermon proper begins with a pre-sermon consisting of a brief analysis of the lesson that leads up to the real sermon. This is the only possible form of introduction. All others are to be rejected in principle.

Certain practical or, if one will, psychological reasons may be advanced against introductions.

i. Why do we come to church? We want to hear the Word of God that comes to us in the sermon, which as explication of the text is also application. The course of worship itself is the introduction to the sermon, its climax. The act of proclamation should begin at once. Any additional introduction is a waste of time. Since a sermon cannot go on too long, it is irresponsible. No doubt introductions offer many opportunities for much wit and cleverness, but in any case too much precious time is wasted by intellectual gymnastics of this kind. Twenty to twenty-five minutes may often be spent on preliminaries before coming to the main point.

Note: The general maxim that brevity is the soul of wit may be true of any form of speech but it should not be applied to the sermon. The task of the sermon is to create space for the Word of God, which alone can be the criterion for the length of the sermon. This is not to deny that sermons might be delivered in a shorter time. We have to realize, however, that exposition is serious worship and is thus the most important part of our Sunday. If we want to honor God, we should not raise the question of time.

ii. The greater part of all introductions does not introduce. It distracts our thoughts from the Word of God. Instead of leading in, it leads out. A purely psychological consideration would already lead us to this conclusion. At the beginning of a sermon the listeners are still in a state of suspense and attentive. If the preacher first converses about something else—maybe something very interesting—it may well happen that one or the other of them will be completely "turned off" when a switch is finally made to the real matter at hand.

iii. What meaning does an introduction have for serious listeners who want to hear a call from God and are ready for it? They will be disappointed in their purpose and their frustration will block their hearing of the message.

What is it that the introduction usually contains?

i. A popular starting point is the present age, which

the pastor views either favorably or unfavorably. Poor sermon introductions of this kind will begin, for example, with the words: "Our age . . ." Either the preacher likes what is going on—and the introduction will be positive—or he does not—and it will be negative. What is forgotten is that the congregation is not asking the preacher for an analysis of the times. They may perhaps know more about such things than the preacher does and the sermon is no place in which to look for them.

ii. Again, the preacher may quote a famous person by way of introduction. But what can this accomplish when the text has been read and prayer offered? The thoughts of the listeners are simply led off in another direction. We need to realize that mere mention of an extraneous name will automatically evoke the most incredible associations of ideas in the hearers, who will then inevitably wander in their own thoughts. The preacher certainly cannot commend the biblical saying or passage by pointing out that someone else once said something similar or dissimilar. This is unworthy of the matter.

iii. Another more serious possibility concerns the introduction that is deliberately given a negative orientation. What is involved? Simply an unmasking of human wickedness and sin. This contemplation of the awful pomp of fallen humanity can never stop. Preachers can never be sated when taking aim at the sin they see entrenched in front of them. But the depiction of sin and error, which offer so rich a field, ought not to take on autonomous significance in a sermon. We have no right to bespatter a Christian congregation, or one that is almost Christian, with such a shower of bitterness from the very outset. The danger then arises that we will be using the Bible only as a club that we swing with mounting passion at sinful humanity. At any event, we will not in this way lead the congregation to

the text. Even to aim at the old Adam in us and then
to oppose to it the great "But" of God is not appropriate. If we first turn the spotlight on humanity in its
corruption, we are then exposed to the danger of a
secret theme in the sermon, with the Bible merely as a
setting. The Word must reveal the error.

iv. There is another serious possibility. Even though
the first three mistakes be recognized and avoided, the
imminent danger exists of prefixing to the sermon
proper a situation report on the content of the text.
Many sermons that are meant to be biblical begin with
some biblical theology, or Old or New Testament introduction, or biblical history. As constituent parts,
such things do not belong in the sermon.

The theological damage of sermon introductions is in
any event incredibly extensive, and it is usually an
error when preachers use them. For what do they really
involve at root? Nothing other than the search for a
point of contact, for an analogue in us which can be a
point of entry for the Word of God. It is believed that
this little door to the inner self must first be found and
opened before it is worthwhile to bring the message.
No! This is plain heresy. Were we to view the fall in the
framework of Roman Catholic theology, along the lines
of prevenient grace or the analogy of being, then an
approximation of humanity to God might be possible.
But if we understand the Bible after the manner of the
Reformers, we know that no such possibility exists.
There is only one exception, the contact which is made,
of course, by the miracle of God from on high. When
the Word has found an entrance into a person, then *God*
has worked the miracle, he alone, without any preparation or assistance of ours. We have simply to approach
people knowing that there is nothing in them that we
can address, no *humanum*, no *analogia entis* of any kind
that we can put in touch with the *divinum*, but only the
one great possibility which has no need of our skills,

which alone is efficacious, and which does not need us as advocates, or even as "detectives," as one modern theologian has called pastors. "The Father has spoken"—only in this way and no other. We have simply to adopt the attitude of the messenger who does not have to create a mood for the message. No doubt all this seems to be wildly destructive of the little garden of our sermon out of which we had hoped to pluck so many blooms!

Preaching cannot try to relate to the divine within us. The miracle must always take place from above. The human listener must be seen and addressed as Adam after the fall, but in the light of the fact that this listener has been called in Christ by baptism. In baptism, however, we have received only the promise, never a point of contact. We are set under the sign of this promise because the saying in John 3:16 is given to *every* human creature as a new foundation . . . that *all* should not perish. This applies even to the most depraved, even to criminals and murderers. A reference to this confidence that on the basis of baptism a miracle has happened to us is the best introduction to every sermon. The fact that we are not speaking to people who are outside but inside will be the irresistible force that a sermon exerts when God grants his grace to this end. What we have here is nothing short of a miracle, but it is the promised miracle. That we humans may speak of this is an incredible thing, and yet it is no more than simple service. We have simply to assume the attitude of a messenger who has something to say. We have no need to build a slowly ascending ramp, for there is no height that we have to reach. No! Something has to come down from above. And this can happen only when the Bible speaks from the very outset. We have then done what we could.

c. *Parts?*

We have already said that the sermon has to be a corpus, a body, not with parts but with members. This requirement is connected with the nature of the homily, i.e., the rejection of the theme sermon, in which a division of thought according to a material or logical principle is a natural consequence. In the homily the text itself must be the decisive factor. The main mistakes that are made when divisions are introduced are as follows.

In the first part faith might be presented as theory, while practice is the subject in the second part. Or the law might be discussed in the first part, the gospel in the second. Divisions of this kind fit in very well, but scripture does not make them; their meaningful place is in dogmatics. It is quite fatal to tear apart explication and application as Schleiermacher does by first developing the text more or less historically and then going on to say: "But we!" It is not even appropriate to speak first about Christ and his dealings with us, and then to apply all that has been said to ourselves.

The proper way is to construct the corpus of the sermon in repetition of the text's own rhythm and with due regard to the proportions discerned by exegesis. In such repetition we need not deal with the passage schematically verse by verse as in the work of preparation. That will sometimes be the appropriate way, but often the decisive point at which to begin will be the middle or the end of the verse or passage. Nor is it necessary to pay equal attention to all the verses. The homily principle involves no bondage to the letter. If the text is unevenly accentuated, allowance must be made for this. Perhaps very little need be said about the letter, but the content must come out at all costs. Finding all this is the business of exegesis. We might take John 1:43–51 as an example. In this case the sermon should center on verses 47f.: Christ knows predestined Nathaniel. Everything else simply leads to this center. The aim of the sermon should not be that people receive a few thoughts but that they open the Bible and note the way of witness that it takes.

d. *Conclusion?*

As we reject the special introduction, so there can be no independent conclusion; the sermon has to end with the exposition. If a summary is needed, it is already too late to give it; the mischief has been done. A theoretical sermon cannot be made more practical by a concluding application. Address can never come too soon. The same applies to a concluding exhortation. Motivating is especially dangerous and seductive: the sounding of a great Hallelujah in the style of Romans 8. As surely as this may sometimes be done, we must be warned against it as a method. The sermon must certainly be worship, but as a whole and not merely at the end. If it is so only at the end, it is no longer credible.

An important, comforting, and critical little word is the "Amen" with which we confess what we have said before God. "Amen" may be a comfort to us after what has been said in weakness. It also causes us to think of the next sermon and summons us back to work. Every sermon thus closes on both a comforting and an unsettling note. From this little word we might unpack the whole doctrine of preaching.

5. Rules for Handling the Text

a. Let us be careful not to snap the thread of the text and intrude something alien to it! We must accept throughout the lordship of the text and thus be on guard against anything we might import into it.

b. It is to be recommended in principle that no statement should be made that is either explication alone or application alone. We should not play the role of the exegete who never deviates from the text. We should never lecture on the text but simply say what is there. This continuous sharpshooting means work. No explication, then, without application, or vice versa!

c. We should not try to master the text. The Bible will become more and more mysterious to real exegetes. They will see all the depths and distances. They will constantly run up against the mystery before which theology is like trying to drain the ocean with a spoon. The true exegete will face the text like an astonished child in a wonderful garden, not like an advocate of God who has seen all his files.

d. No exegete should stand in the pulpit wondering whether a word is to be understood this way or that. That is part of the preparatory work that belongs in the study. The congregation should be presented with the *results* of this careful preparatory work.

e. Though explication is application, this does not mean that a present-day meaning has to be stated at all costs. A sermon can often be more relevant when it does not seem to be relevant at all. Hence we should never expressly state and affirm that this is what holy scripture means for us today. The meaning is to be presupposed as self-evident.

6. The Problem of Language

Sermons are often said to be "too lofty," i.e., too abstract, too theological. Now we do not want to suggest that theology is something very lofty and that we have to stoop down to the poor folk below. Nevertheless, for all the dilution there still exists a sense that something very serious has to be passed on in preaching. In most cases trivialities are undoubtedly the result of laziness. We ought to preach earnestly. The seriousness of the matter and the seriousness of life demand it.

It is natural that our individuality and situation should come to expression in our language—but we should also try to remember that we are to speak as servants. We may make our own curves around the great curve of the text, but these can never seek to have a life of their own either in us or in our listeners. We must be cautious, then, in our use of images and parallels, which will be good only if we keep a strong discipline. The danger is especially acute when we present personal experiences. We must also be careful not to intrude into the lives of the listeners. The silence that usually descends if we do is a loaded silence. At this point especially we need to remember that the pulpit is the place where we have to obey orders.

7. Discussions of Two Sermons

a. *Sermon on Luke 9:57–58* * *by Mr. J.*

Contents. The sermon is based on very specific interpretations of the text. As regards verse 57, it is assumed that the offer of discipleship is completely valid. The issue is thought to be the hard and difficult road that Jesus is taking, namely to Jerusalem. This is a difficult road because in contrast to our little faith it demands a strongly believing heart. Final seriousness finds expression here because Jesus is going up to Jerusalem to the cross. As regards verse 58, the point is made that everything depends on our seeing and believing the

---

* [57]As they were going along the road, someone said to him, "I will follow you wherever you go."

[58]And Jesus said to him, "Foxes have holes, and birds of the air have nests; but the Son of Man has nowhere to lay his head."

revelation of God in the poverty of Jesus Christ. Here is someone who has no anxiety, whose place is beyond the world, but the world does not understand this. Thus the kingdom of God stands in antithesis to us. The world crucifies Christ, and with this very act the kingdom of God is proclaimed and revealed. This proclamation, that Christ in his poverty is present to us, is the gospel. This and not the world is the final word. We face the question whether or not we hear the great Yes of this message in the No—and this links the sermon to its starting point. Here is the decision that we have to make.

Discussion. [Three strong points were emphasized first.]

i. The exposition of the text is an attempt to express the total content of the passage, e.g., the unity of law and gospel, or the exposition of verse 57 in terms of verse 58.

ii. The preacher succeeded in bringing to our notice what we had heard, namely that following Jesus is a serious task, that it is the way to the cross, radical negative theology, and as such law and gospel.

iii. Finally, it should not fail to be noted that we have been addressed with sincere religious zeal.

[The weak points of the sermon were discussed more fully.] Above all, the sermon lacks closeness to life. The explication does not become application. No claim is made, no challenge. The transition from verse 57 to verse 58 is no real step. Is the text alone to blame for this, or the sermon? With this question we should also ask: Was the religious zeal Christian zeal? Was the clarity of the sermon the clarity of the divine Word? Is the attempt to let the text speak really successful? It is the exegesis that decides this. When discussing the exegesis we have to ask first whether the offer of discipleship was in fact a valid one in this case. But it is inappropriate to settle this question either negatively or

positively. Our only response has to be silence. At all
events the question remains an open one, and elucidation can be found only from verse 58. On this basis
three things must be said.

(a) If the *akolouthēsō soi* ("I will follow you") is valid,
this obviously means that the man has to say it in
obedience to a command, and he thus had knowledge
of Jesus because he has heard his voice. But in this case
discipleship already means acknowledgment, and the
question of the great No and Yes has already been
answered. The following derives from what has already
been said, that is: I have been freed by him who has
nowhere to lay his head. I have been freed from having
to find a place where I must pronounce the great No
and Yes together. I am relieved of this necessity. I am
not a Platonist, for the Platonist has to have that place
beyond the Yes and No. He has a place to lay his head.
This burden of decision is taken from this man. He is
no longer homeless, without a place to stand, but a
comforted and directed wanderer. Thus, if his offer is
valid, he already stands in faith and obedience.

(b) If, however, the offer is not valid, it would mean
that this man has a high ideal of life—perhaps a Pla-
tonic one—and has engraved on it the image of Jesus.
From him he expects the fulfillment of this ideal, which
means that there is a possibility of discipleship—"one
can." It is a great mistake to think that we can make our
own decision for God. Armored with ideals and
trapped in this error, we seek a home for ourselves in
the best sense. But in so doing we miss the real libera-
tion by the incarnate Word that is offered to us in Jesus.

(c) The question of validity must be posed in terms
of verse 58. On earth Jesus Christ is flesh, but he does
not come of flesh (John 1:14; Heb. 13:14; the virgin
birth). Jesus Christ is there for us as the Word of God
(*in* the world but not *of* it), as the Word of the Father
for the world. This whence and whither leave him no

will of his own. He has no place to lay his head, no nest in which to rest, as we have. Discipleship means accepting and acknowledging this man who is wholly from God and who has been sent for us. It means letting him be given us. To be obedient here means to believe. Not to follow is not to be obedient, not to believe. It means wanting to help oneself.

The sermon might be preached in this sequence. In any case it would be totally wrong to begin with the negation, with the destruction, as in the sequence (b, a, c). The best sequence would be (c, b, a): In light of this exegesis even the good qualities of the sermon might be called into question.

b. *Sermon on Luke 9:59–60* * *by Mr. H.*

Contents. The preacher begins with the contrast between verse 59a, the demand for discipleship, and verse 57, the voluntary offer. It brings out sharply the claim of Jesus. No excuse is possible, no tie to earthly things, nor even to the divine commandment: "Honor father and mother." Verse 60b then shows what is the task of proclamation, with no earthly tie to be sure, yet full of promise.

Discussion. The following strong points may be noted. First, an effort is made at good exposition. Second, a whole series of biblical insights is expressed. Finally, the language is simple and unembellished.

But the sermon also has serious weaknesses. Its brevity does not seem to be justified. Verse 60b is not properly treated. Furthermore, verses 59, 60a, and 60b fall totally apart, so that the sermon lacks unity. Finally, the preacher passes by too quickly the question of the

---

* [59]To another he said, "Follow me." But he said, "Lord, first let me go and bury my father."

[60]But Jesus said to him, "Let the dead bury their own dead; but as for you, go and proclaim the kingdom of God."

command. What does Jesus mean: "Let the dead bury their dead"? It must be asked, then, whether the partially good exposition is really exposition of this text. Are the good biblical insights really won from this text or have they been added to it? Here again exegesis must decide.

(a) The "Follow me" is an irresistible demand. It means: "I will act for you." No rights, no cares, no responsibility, no dominion of one's own—this is what it means to have a master.

(b) In face of this there can be no *prōton* ("first let me go . . ."). Ministry begins at once or not at all. Neither legitimate reasons of piety nor even the orders of creation may interfere. These have their validity, but within this "Follow me" and not in themselves, as no longer independent but dependent concerns. The command of Jesus takes precedence.

(c) Following means "life." The orders of natural life are the orders of a displaced world. They are valid only when adopted in hope.

(d) Proclamation of the kingdom of God is the concrete mission that this man is given, and it demands every sacrifice. The kingdom of God means the limiting of everything that we regard as commanded. Thus a shadow falls over the earthly things that we take for granted, but also a light of hope for this world of the provisional. This proclamation must have priority as depicted.

It would be best to preach the sermon in the sequence (d, c, b, a) or (d, a, b, c), but in any case not (b, a, c, d), which would put the negation first.

8. Appendix

a. If a question is raised in conclusion, it should be meant only as proclamation and never as a new problem relating to a questionable opinion.

b. As regards free prayer after the sermon, it is often mere babble which gives the impression that the preacher is not prepared. That should not be.

c. It is not out of keeping with the good news that the sermon should be read. About this there are different opinions in different quarters. The main point is that what is done should be right and responsible.

d. Verses of hymns as the finale are to be judged in the same way as the Hallelujah ending. There must be good reasons for quoting in a sermon.

[The final meeting of the seminar closed with a warning against theological bias, a simple repetition of the principles of dialectical theology, and a summons to ever new listening to the Word of scripture concerning the reconciliation that took place in Jesus Christ.]

Postscript

In the summer semester of 1965, under the title *Wesen und Vorbereitung der Predigt* (Nature and Preparation of the Sermon), the present *Homiletik* came out in duplicated form for theological students at Bonn. It might be helpful to give some account of how this text took shape.

Just before the beginning of the 1965 summer semester, while looking for books on homiletics, with the help of students and teachers at Bonn in the theological seminar I came across a collection of records of the homiletical seminar on "Exercises in Sermon Preparation" which Karl Barth had held in Bonn in the winter semester of 1932 and the summer semester of 1933. Already on a first reading I thought of duplicating these, and I was encouraged to do this by conversations with the instructors, by the contribution of Professor Walther Fürst of Friedberg (a seminar participant in the winter of 1932) to the *Barth-Festschrift Antwort* ("Karl Barths Predigtlehre" ["Karl Barth's Doctrine of Preaching," pp. 137ff.), and by the recommendation that Professor Fürst kindly sent me for the prospectus that I was circulating.

In this prospectus we read: "The question of the responsibility of preachers is the starting point and goal of the theology of Karl Barth from its inception. It is no wonder then, that the homiletical colloquium that he held in the years 1932–1933 dealt most intensively with that issue. In it he clarified many of the problems which he discussed only later in his *Dogmatics,* e.g., the relation of gospel and law, or the question of the relation of the church to the world. The freshness and joy that we can still detect in the transcripts today put the listeners of that time so firmly on the path that they could tread it with sure steps even through the confusing times that were then dawning and that Barth could clearly see coming. We must be grateful that these *Exercises* are being made available to a wider public. Though Barth later modified and corrected many things, they have even today an astonishing relevance."

The editing of these records was made possible by the friendly consent of Professor Barth and the support of the Bonn teachers. The official "protocols" read in the seminar form the basis of this manuscript. These have been compared with the transcripts and the style smoothed out where necessary. To a large extent parts of a transcript acquired from Werner Deggeller have been used from Part 3 ("Actual Preparation of the Sermon") onward. The title and some of the headings have been reformulated for material reasons. The text has also been put in sections arranged according to the key words.

It is at the wish of Professor Barth, communicated to me by Professor Max Geiger, that this expanded and revised text now appears in print. It has been thoroughly worked over afresh for this purpose.

In book form Barth's doctrine of preaching will undoubtedly find grateful readers and evoke joy and courage for the proper proclamation of the gospel.

GÜNTER SEYFFERTH

Bonn, January 1966